INTERNATIONAL COLONY KURDISTAN

İsmail Beşikçi

Gomidas Institute
London

International Colony Kurdistan (Devletlerarası Sömürge Kürdistan) was originally published in Turkish by Alan Yayıncılık in 1990. The present work is an authorised translation from the Turkish original. It was first published under the Gomidas Institute's "Parvana" imprint (2004).

ISBN 978-1-909382-20-6

Gomidas Institute
42 Blythe Rd.
London W14 0HA
England
Email: *info@gomidas.org*
Web: *www.gomidas.org*

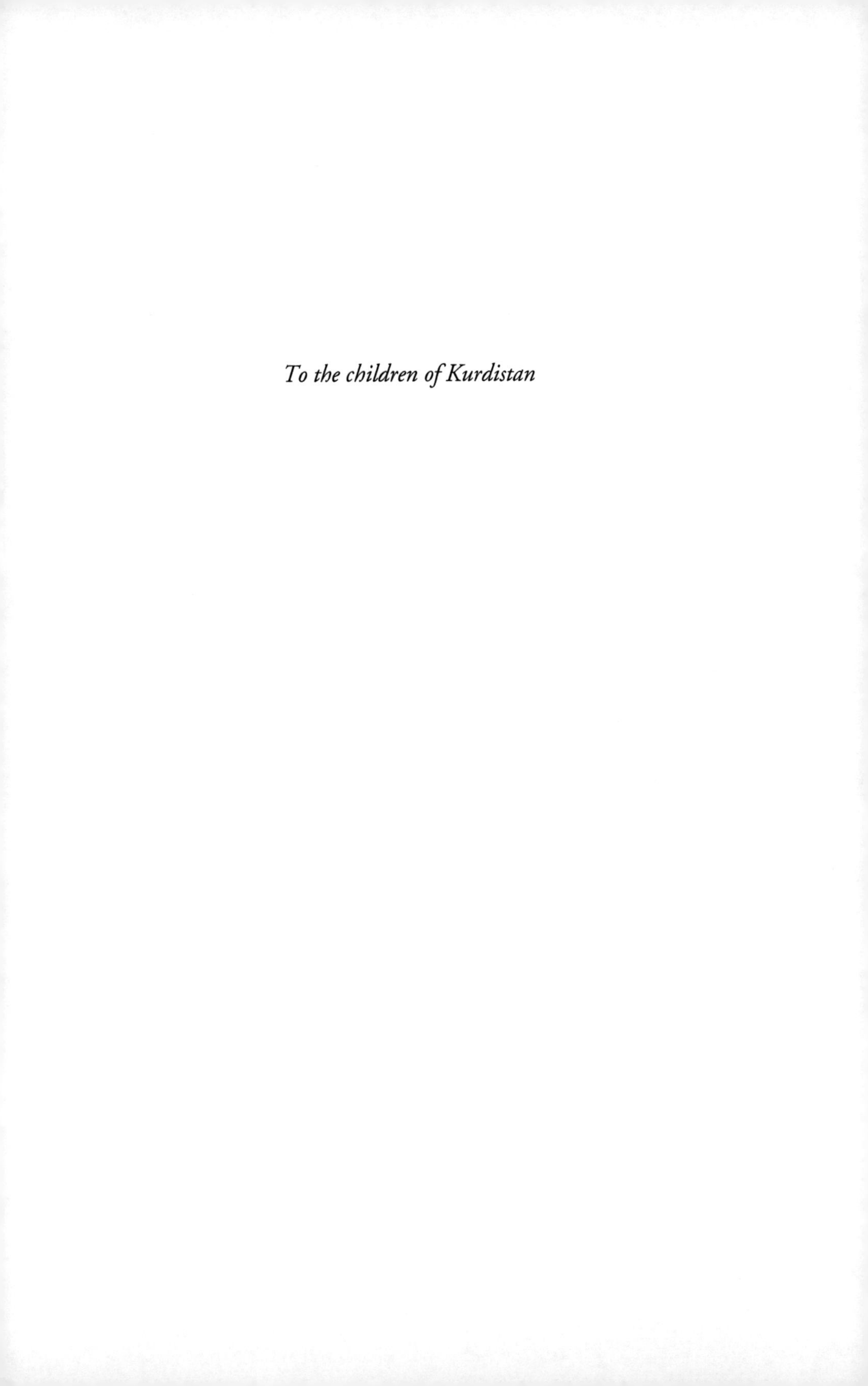

To the children of Kurdistan

Foreword to English Edition

Currently, a serious issue looms large on the agendas of Turkey, Iran, Iraq, Syria, and increasingly in the United States, Europe, and Russia: the problem of Kurds and Kurdistan. What exactly is this problem? The issue concerns the disintegration, break up, and partitioning of Kurds and their lands in the 1920s—during the era of the League of Nations—and the usurpation of their right to independent statehood. It is a process that was enabled by the collaboration of the two imperial states of the time, Great Britain and France, with long-established states under Turkish, Persian, and Arab administrations in the Middle East. Thus, during the era of the League of Nations, a new status quo was established that granted no status to Kurds and Kurdistan.

The League of Nations was founded at the end of World War I for the purpose of a peaceful resolution to international discord without recourse to war. The right of nations to self-determination was widely debated both in the Soviet Union and the United States, and many regions of the world struggled to realise it. Lenin, Stalin and Trotsky in the Soviet Union and President Roosevelt in the United States often alluded to this principle. However, Kurds and Kurdistan remained disintegrated, broken apart and partitioned. Every part of Kurdistan was annexed by a different state and in most places, the words "Kurds" and "Kurdistan," and the Kurdish language itself were prohibited.

This spelled out an international order defined by a fundamental anti-Kurdishness. In the 1920s, 30s, and 40s, this anti-Kurdish international order was overseen by Great Britain and France, along with Turkey and Iran. After World War II, Great Britain handed over Iraq—and thus, Kurdistan—to Iraq, while France handed Syria—and thus, Kurdistan—over to Syria. Henceforth, Kurdistan was co-governed by Turkey, Iran, Iraq, and Syria, with assistance from such states as Great Britain, France, and the United States. The Soviet Union lent much support to the anti-Kurdish international order, standing firm against any status concerning Kurds and taking the side of states that together oppressed the Kurds and Kurdistan.

In 1918-19, Shaikh Mahmud Berzenji of Southern Kurdistan told British authorities, "I am the king of Kurdistan, recognise me as the king of Kurdistan." But the imperial powers did not envision even a colonised Kurdistan, let alone an independent Kurdish state. When the lands of the Ottoman Empire in the Middle East were being partitioned, British mandates were formed in Iraq, Jordan, and Palestine, and French mandates in Syria and Lebanon, but Kurdistan was never founded. One has to ask why no Kurdistan was not formed and why the lands of Kurds were disintegrated, torn apart, and partitioned.

The League of Nations was unable to deliver international peace as expected and could not prevent the outbreak of the Second World War. The Kurds stood firm during this war, as the western region of Iran was invaded by the Soviet Union and Great Britain in 1941. The Kurdish national movement flourished in Mahabad, in the territory invaded by the Soviet Union. In 1946, the Mahabad Kurdistan Republic was erected but could only last for a year. As a result of the withdrawal of the Soviet Union and the Soviet-Iran treaty, the region again came under Iranian control. The leaders of the Republic of Mahabad-Kurdistan, President Kadi Muhammed, and the ministers were executed.

The reinstatement of international peace and the need for a supra-state organisation was on statesmen's mind during the Second World War as well. The United Nations was founded in 1945 for this purpose. The emphasis during the founding of the United Nations was on the incompetence and flaws of the League of Nations and the need to remedy them. In the post-1945 period, Kurds made much effort to make their voices heard to the founders of the United Nations, but their cries went unheeded. The League of Nations, the United Nations… these organizations with the word "Nations" in their names… have never safeguarded the rights of all nations, but always taken the side of nations that have oppressed others.

After the Second World War, there were many major political changes in the world. For instance, the colonies in Africa gained independence one by one after the 1960s. But no such change took place in Kurdistan. The status quo that denied any status to Kurdistan was preserved in the era of the United Nations. Kurdistan was not even a colony. If it were, it would have had borders. There would have been a definite country described by such phrases as "India, the British colony," "Algeria, the French colony," "Angola, the Portuguese colony." No such situation applied to Kurdistan.

The United Nations "Declaration on the Granting of Independence to Colonial Countries and Peoples," Number 1514 (XV) on 14 December

1960 should be considered differently for overseas colonies and border colonies. While clauses 1, 2, 3, and 5 of this seven-clause decision encouraged the independence of overseas colonies, clauses 4, 6, and 7 encouraged the prevention and suppression of decolonisation and liberation movements in border colonies.

Colonies are often ruled by oppression, tyranny, and violence. In which colonies are oppression, tyranny, and violence more prevalent? In overseas colonies or in bordering colonies? In which colonies is genocide perpetrated and toxic gas used? Has such a thing as the genocide of Kurds in Halabja in March 1988 occurred in overseas colonies?

How is this lack of status for Kurds and Kurdistan reflected in our day? Today, in the European Union of 28 member states, Luxembourg, Cyprus, and Malta are nations with populations of less than a million each. Luxembourg and Malta have half a million citizens each. In Cyprus, the Greeks and Turks combined number just over a million. But these countries are member states of the European Union, the European Council, the United Nations, and the Organisation for Security and Co-operation in Europe. Yet Kurds, with a population of 40-50 million, lack political status. This fundamental anomaly in international relations must surely be addressed on ample factual grounds. Other states among the 28 members of the European Union, such as Estonia, Latonia, Lithuania, Slovenia, and Slovakia have populations of two to three million.

Only five of 28 member states of the European Union have populations greater than that of the Kurds in the Middle East: Germany, France, Great Britain, Italy, and Spain. Poland has a population perhaps equal to the total population of Kurdistan; the populations of the rest of the states in the European Union are far less than the total Kurdish population.

We could also consider the European Council of 47 member states, where the populations of four countries—Andorra, San Marino, Monaco, and Liechtenstein—vary between 30 and 40 thousand. These states are members of the United Nations and of the Organization for Security and Co-operation in Europe. They participate in all sorts of sporting competitions such as the Olympics, the World Cup, the UEFA Champions League, etc. The Kurds, on the other hand, with their population of 40-50 million, lack any political status whatsoever. They are not equal members in the world family of nations, although there are strong grounds that they should be. Their exclusion reflects the depth and prevalence of the anti-Kurdish international order.

Without mentioning the fact that tiny states like Andorra, San Marino, Monaco, and Liechtenstein have not had to pay a price for their freedom, Kurds have been paying dearly for their continued existence as a people. They have suffered oppression, tyranny, and genocides. One may use the word "millions" as the price they have paid, in human lives, for their freedom, homeland, and national liberation since the nineteenth century.

Today, there are many states with a population of under one million in the Islamic Congress (57 members) and in the United Nations (193 members). In the Pacific, off Australia and New Zealand, the states named Tuvalu, Vanuatu, and Kiribati have populations that vary between ten and fifteen thousand. These states are also represented, for instance, in the Olympics, which shows that they are members of the family of world nations. The Kurds, however, despite their large numbers, are not represented in international competitions, reminding us that they are not equal members in the family of world nations. Significant effort must be made to change these injustices.

States such as Kuwait, Qatar, Bahrain, and the United Arab Emirates in the Gulf of Basra and Djibouti on the shores of the Red Sea have populations of under one million. Due to the events that began in Syria in March 2011, three states are often mentioned as regional actors: Turkey, Saudi Arabia, Qatar... Since March 2011 the Kurds have been striving in Rojava in the southwest of Kurdistan to establish an autonomous government of Kurdistan. These three states are at great pains to prevent the establishment of such an autonomous government and arm organizations within the Free Syrian Army such as al-Qaeda, al-Nusra Front and the Islamic State of Iraq and Syria (ISIS), all the while claiming, "there is no Kurdistan in Syria." Among these three states, Qatar has come to have a major role in determining the future of the Kurds—Qatar, which is a state in the Gulf of Basra with a population of under 300 thousand. Why is such a state so decisive in determining the destiny of the Kurds? Yet another dimension of the anti-Kurdish international world order.

One must also offer an explanation concerning a Kurdish population of 40 or 50 million people in the Middle East. Nowhere has the population of Kurds been clearly established, neither in Turkey, nor in Iran, Iraq, Syria. When taking these four states into account, one must not forget the Kurds of the Caucasus. What has become of the Red Kurdistan which came into being in 1923-29? Located between today's Armenia and Nagorny Karabagh, that land included the cities of Qelbejer, Lachin, Kubatli, Zengilan, and Jebrail. The abolition of Red Kurdistan in 1930 and the forced exile of the Kurds to Central Asian republics such as

Kyrgyzstan, Kazakhstan and Uzbekistan also deserves greater attention, as does the capture of Red Kurdistan by the Karabagh Armenians in the Armenian-Azerbaijani war over Nagorny Karabagh in the 1990s

The first edition of *International Colony Kurdistan* (translated from the Turkish original, *Devletlararası Sömürge, Kürdistan*) came out in the 1990s. Back then, we maintained that the Kurdish issue was a momentous one, in fact the most important issue facing Turkey. Today, the question of Kurds and Kurdistan remains a major issue, not only in Turkey, but also in Iran, Iraq, and Syria, as well as further afield in the U.S.A., the European Union, and the Russian Federation. The Kurdish issue has a large share in the development of the ISIS and has been the catalyst in the internationalisation of the ISIS problem.

There has been much research and analysis concerning Kurds, Kurdistan and Kurdish since the 1990s, and this process continues in full gear. Such research has also drawn attention to Kurdish relations with Armenians, Assyrians-Suryanis, Yazidi Kurds, Jews, and others. It is high time for new research and reflection to include not only on Kurdish-Arabic-Turkish-Persian relations, but also Kurdish-Armenian-Assyrian/ Suryani relations, as well as those between Kurdistan and Armenia.

İsmail Beşikçi
15 August, 2015

1. *Red Kurdistan (1923)*
2. *Kurdish Republic of Mahabad (1946)*
3. *Kurdish Autonomous Region of Iraq (1975)*
4. *Greater Kukrdistan (claimed at UN, 1945)*

GEORGIA
Tbilisi
AZERBAIJAN
ARMENIA
L. Sevan
Kars
Yerevan
Igdir
Artsakh
(Nagorno-
Karabagh)
1
L. Van
Van
Siirt
Khoy
Tabriz
L. Urmieh
IRAN
2
Mahabad
Zakho
Dohuk
Mosul
3
Arbil
IRAQ
Kerkuk
Halabjah
Sanandaj
N
W
E
S
100
200 km. approx.

Introduction to English Edition

At a time when humans can walk on the moon and aspire to reach the stars how could one imagine a colony called Kurdistan? Indeed, those who control it would like you to think that it does not exist at all. Therein lies the importance of the present publication as a contribution not only to our understanding of Kurds and Kurdistan, but also of our earth and its myriad peoples wondering aimlessly and sometimes dangerously on it. This flickering light on this much-neglected issue is timely, revealing, and also disquieting. Looking at what it reveals, I could not help but remember the time when the Taliban mercilessly attacked the stone statue of Buddha in Afghanistan. With the exception of a few gaping art critics, not much was said about the pulverizing assault on art. The emboldened attackers then attacked the Twin Towers in New York City. It then became fashionable to say that, had the world kept a closer tab on these misguided "true believers" with turbans in Kabul, perhaps the tragedy of September 11 could have been averted.

A similar assault is now taking place on a people, called Kurds, on a land, called Kurdistan, and again with the exception of a few, this time gaping Kurds, no one is bothered with this misuse and abuse of power against a defenseless people and their land. The arts, thank God, have their protectors dispersed all over the world, the Kurds, unfortunately, do not prompt such a defense. The world, one day, could indeed witness the days, like what befell the stone statues of Buddha in Afghanistan, the pulverization of Kurds and Kurdistan. And if these molesters of the Kurds do not export their violence abroad, especially to the countries in the Occident—no such plans have ever been uttered by the abusers of the Kurds so far—few will hear and fewer still will read about the tragedy that befell the Kurds, notwithstanding the recent war in Iraq, unless, of course, the Kurds and their friends do something, now, about the merciless attack on their very existence that goes on unabated throughout the Middle East.

That something was done by Dr. Beşikçi in this book you are holding in your hands—and many others that have yet to be translated—is beyond any question. The treatment Dr. Beşikçi received in Turkey makes it abundantly clear that he was viewed with hatred, persecuted with diligence, and branded as an enemy of the state or a darling of all those who are the sworn enemies of the Turks. He did—a better word for it would be "tried"—what thousands of undergraduate, graduate and doctoral students do all over the world—except unfortunately in places like Turkey, Syria, Iraq, and Iran—to study the Kurds. For his efforts, harassment became his lot from his Turkish compatriots; torture, often meted by Kurdish guards, became his companion; and jail become his home in 13 different places. And yes, at one time, his prison sentences were in the vicinity of three digits, until an amnesty released him from his latest abode, in 1999, and by then, he had served 17 of them behind bars.

The western readers who draw solace in benign concepts such as "cultural relativism" and the "sovereignty of states" often remain indifferent and can't be bothered with what the Turks, Arabs and Persians are doing to the Kurds. But indifference was not one of Mr. Beşikçi's faults. At the age of 22, in 1961, he headed, as an intern, to Elazig, a predominantly Kurdish city in Turkish misruled Kurdistan, and to his surprise uncovered a lie that his government had been trying, assiduously, to hide from him and his compatriots for the past 38 years. The lie was that everybody in Turkey was a Turk. So when the young Beşikçi came face to face with the Kurds in Turkey, he did not, to be sure, like the ancient Greek mathematician Archimedes, run out of the governor's office, the place of his work, to shout eureka, eureka, eureka, or the Turkish version, buldum, buldum, buldum, but observed a profoundly cowed and frightened population who had to use the help of translators to communicate with his boss. Something snapped in Mr. Beşikçi there and then. The Kurds acquired a friend in this diminutive yet steely man. The Turks, lucky for them, put on the path of truth, one of their own.

So how do you go around with a mission like discovering truth about the Kurds in a country like Turkey that claims, even today, it has no Kurds of its own, see Article 66 of the Turkish constitution. That same constitution, under the subsection of freedom of expression and dissemination of thought, no less, makes a reference to a "prohibited language," read Kurdish, and how it shall not be allowed for use to express or disseminate information, see Article 26. That some constitution—a psychiatrist would have a field day reading it—makes 22 references to, "the indivisible integrity of the state with its territory and people," which only underscores the very existence of peoples other than Turks in that forsaken peninsula and the very real possibility of separation if it were possible for these peoples to express their will without the fear of persecution. That same constitution, in going to the lengths that it does about the "unitary" nature of the state, only holds a mirror to the level of contempt that Turks hold towards Kurds and other minorities, for that matter, and the upshot is a monstrosity worthy of horror movies that goes by the name of a government.

The most jarring example of this denial of the Kurds—perhaps it is not a coincidence—has found its most poignant expression in the English playwright Harold Pinter's play, "The Language of the Mountains," notes Dr. Beşikçi. The reference is to another lie in the Turkish nomenclature, unique in the annals of history, where Kurds are referred to as mountain Turks. In the play, a Kurdish activist is arrested and imprisoned. His mother wants to visit him, and is told that she will not be able to speak her mountain language, but only the state sanctioned one, Turkish. The trouble is, she doesn't even know how to speak Turkish. So she goes to the prison anyway, and the most she can do is stare at her son. In a second visit, the mother is told that an exception has been made to the prohibition and that she can now speak her "mountain language," but this time, she refuses to speak. Rage and fury emanate from her eyes and face, but no words will crack her mouth. Her son's pleadings are worthless. She has decided to do what she wants to do and be no part of a state that has only disdained her. Inside the prison, a rebel Kurd is born.

One could perhaps applaud this imaginary Kurdish mother, apparently prompted by a real one, who found a way to bedevil the Turks even though submitting to them would have been what a mother would do for the love of her son. The Turks may not know it, but their behavior only resonates with what the Nazi leader, Herman Goering, used to say, "When I hear the word culture, I reach out to my revolver." Such brutality is the norm in Turkey and has created, what Mr. Beşikçi calls, a predominantly "cowardly," "submissive," and "obedient" Kurdish population. The Turks seem content with their progress and often brag about the compliance of their subjects. And it looks like it is not just the former Nazis who would offer kudos to the Turks, but last June, this Kurd was horror-struck to read in the Turkish press that the United Nations too had decided to cheer Turkey on with its campaign of cultural genocide against the Kurds.

The story was in the *Turkish Daily News.* It ran on June 18, 2003. It was titled, "Education Campaign Kicks Off in Southeast." The drive was part of the United Nations' Children Fund (UNICEF) drive to ensure that Turkey would "Leave No Child Behind." UNICEF Executive Director Carol Bellamy was at hand in Van to bless the undertaking in person and sanctify it with the name of her employer, the United Nations. All that, on the face of it at least, looks good. Who could, in his or her right mind, be against education? But the thought lingered, would Turks do anything good for the Kurds? Can a deer expect mercy from a wolf?

The article noted that there were 7 million illiterate people in Turkey, and 6 million of these were women. It went on to say that the campaign would target the cities of Van, Ağrı, Batman, Bitlis, Diyarbekir, Hakkarı, Muş, Siirt, Şanlıurfa and Şirnak. But the article did not bother to note that all these cities are situated in the heart of Turkish Kurdistan. It did not address the discrepancy of why all these illiterate children, millions of them, were concentrated in the Kurdish regions alone. And it made no reference, whatsoever, to what would be taught in these schools to the Kurdish children. Ms. Bellamy noted, the scene must have tickled the Turks, "Our aim is to convince families to allow their girls to attend and finish eight-year compulsory education."

Dr. Beşikçi calls these same compulsory Turkish schools torture chambers for Kurdish children. This scribbler remembers vividly how, he and his classmates were often terrorized in these same schools, back in the 1960s, by Turkish teachers who ran them like indoctrination camps. The mornings would begin with the ubiquitous pledge of allegiance that would end with, "varlığım, Türk varlığına armağan olsun," which translates to something like, may my life be dedicated to the preservation of the Turkish existence! If one of the students had forgotten to clip his or her nails, mercy would escape the room, and those tiny fingers would get a through beating. If the homework was incomplete, even God would not intervene, the beating would graduate to the form of blows to the face with open hands, the buttocks with kicks, and some of the kids would wet themselves in front of a class full of other children. The body heals, the pain goes away, but the scenes of mortifications endure, and I suspect they will only part us when we are on the other side of the grave. Dr. Beşikçi does a good job of covering these deformities of the Turkish education system, but I doubt very much if any of his findings have ever made it to the desk of Ms. Bellamy. That is why it is of paramount importance to have this book in the English language right now.

The pages of brutality are also interspersed with contradictions that are a prominent feature of Turkey and its inhabitants. The very name, independent Turkey, in any polite and intelligent gathering, conjures up images of the first country that threw off, successfully, the yoke of colonialism and imperialism, says Dr. Beşikçi. Many Turks, to date, ardently believe that, Ataturk, the founder of their country, inspired people like Mahatma Gandhi, Fidel Castro, Ho Chi Mihn, and Nelson Mandela. The latter was awarded Turkey's highest civilian award—no surprise here, the Ataturk prize—in 1992, in the midst of Turkey's genocidal war on the Kurds, but the award was soundly rejected by the African National Congress. The Turks, not knowing what hit them, called Mr. Mandela a cannibal. It may surprise the Turks but a better comparison for their leader would be Adolph Hitler, his contemporary, and closer to home, Saddam Hussein, the butcher of Baghdad, whose statues came tumbling down in Iraqi Kurdistan as soon as he retreated to his lair. If the Turks are wondering what will happen to the statues of Ataturk in Turkish Kurdistan when the Kurds are free to express themselves, the fate that befell the thug from Tikrit may be instructive for them.

Utter the words, independent Kurdistan, says Dr. Beşikçi, in the same polished and courteous Turkish circles that equate Ataturk with Mandela, then expect to be yelled at as "primitive nationalist," tool of "foreign powers," and—you will love this—"minority racist." So it is not just the laws that deny the Kurds a say in the body politic, but the entire Turkish population has been schooled as such that the Kurds are viewed as bad news, especially when they ask for their rights, and the only good ones are those who accept their lot.

Another theme that strikes you throughout the book is the lack of scientific knowledge about the Kurds. The Turks, the Arabs, and the Persians will not engage in such studies notes Dr. Beşikçi, and he urges the Kurds to do so in spite of the odds, and despite the lengthy prison terms. The nascent Kurdish struggle that was unfolding on the mountains of Kurdistan, circa 1990, under the leadership of Abdullah Ocalan wins his praise, and he urges further study of it, and one wonders what he would think of it today, given that Mr. Ocalan himself has now joined the Turkish nationalists in accusing the Kurds who ask for the right of self-determination as "primitive nationalists." Dr. Beşikçi's own analysis and conclusions leave one with no doubt that he favors divorce for the Kurds from the Turks, the Arabs, and the Persians. Only that could restore them their lost dignity, he intones. Only then the Kurds could free themselves of the yokes of cowardice, blind obedience, and submissiveness.

The light that Dr. Beşikçi sheds on the Kurds and Kurdistan may not be very strong, but it is the best that can be shed on them given his circumstances. More is needed, and hopefully, the readers, while understanding Dr. Beşikçi's constraints, will appreciative his efforts to tread on this less travelled road. On his shoulders, to paraphrase Isaac

Newton, you will see a bleeding Kurdistan, a cornered deer if you will, surrounded by wolf, coyote, and jackal. Darkness has enabled the latter to indulge in their assaults; light will serve, especially, the Kurds and Kurdistan on the path of freedom.

Kani Xulam*
Washington DC
July 2003

* Kani Xulam is the director of the American Kurdish Information Network (AKIN),
2600 Connecticut Avenue NW # 1,
Washington, DC 20008, USA

INTERNATIONAL COLONY KURDISTAN

CONTENTS

PART II. Reflections on the "Kurdish Ruling Class"

Appended Materials to English Translation

Part I

Kurdistan and Kurdish Identity

Introduction

1971 was a time of mass arrests and trials. A large number of persons from all sectors of Kurdish society were detained in martial law jails, among them students, peasants, traders, workers, professionals, petty officials, large landowners, sheikhs, and tribal chieftains. The appointed military prosecutors at the Martial Law headquarters of Diyarbekir and Siirt Provinces repeated the standard position prescribed by the official Turkish state ideology over and over like a worn out record. Persons who spoke Kurdish and not even one word of Turkish were said to be Turks, despite the fact that the courts were forced to hire interpreters to communicate with the accused. It was claimed that no such language as Kurdish existed and that the language referred to as Kurdish was no more than a dialect of Turkish. Such views, reported to be the findings of the latest scientific investigations, were enthusiastically defended by authorities from professors to prosecutors. The irreconcilable contradictions between these claims and reality formed one of the basic dimensions of the 1971 Eastern Trials, which opened up a significant new chapter in Kurdish history. Throughout the duration of the trials, Kurds began to reflect on the meaning of their own identity, such as Kurdish nationhood, Kurdish society, Kurdish history, Kurdish language, Kurdish culture, Kurdish literature, and Kurdistan. The process of reflecting, comprehending, and passing on knowledge quickly spread and intensified following the experience of detention, trial, and imprisonment. The most important mass organizations in the East at this time were the Revolutionary Cultural Association of the East and the (underground) Democratic Party of Turkish Kurdistan.

One of the most important products of this process, the development of the thesis on the colonization of Kurdistan and the Kurdish people, emerged in the mid-1970s. From 1974-75 onwards, the thesis that Kurdistan was a colony and the Kurds a colonized nation began to be adopted and developed by nearly all Kurdish organizations as well as some Turkish ones. Soon, these views were being consciously and resolutely defended by wide sectors of Kurdish society, especially the youth.

In the eighties, knowledge on Kurdistan became more widespread, and these developments had a significant influence on the thinking, attitudes, and actions of Kurds. One incident which clearly illustrated the changes undergone in Kurdish society was the fact that during the 1971 Eastern Trials Kurds tried to explain to the courts that Kurdish was a language separate from Turkish, while in the 1980s they actually spoke Kurdish and resolutely defended their position throughout their trials.

This work aims at taking a closer look at Kurdish society in Turkey, in the Middle East, and in the world. It argues that Kurdistan can not be considered a simple colony, and Kurds can not be understood simply as a colonized people. The Kurdish nation was colonized and reduced to a position that is lower than a colony. Such ideas certainly need to be further examined elsewhere. This work is merely an attempt to draw attention to some aspects of these issues and raise a number of pertinent questions.

The Establishment of Colonies in the Nineteenth Century

The history of colonialism separates colonies into two main groups: full colonies and semi-colonies. Full colonies are societies which have not yet reached the stage of founding a state. The capitalist state, in the process of expanding and taking on imperialist qualities, subjects the economy of a traditional society under its domination to its own economy. To facilitate such exploitation politically, a particular order is established in the colonized lands. This order is undoubtedly the product of the imperialist or colonial power, and under the latter's political, administrative, military, cultural, and economic control. Administrators known as Governors, Inspectors, Regents and Viceroys are placed at the heads of bodies through which the colonial power rules the colony. As this organization establishes sovereignty over a specific territory, it is possible to speak of the resulting entity as a "colonial state."

Great Britain's relations with India, Ceylon, Malaysia and Burma in Asia; Kenya, Uganda, Somalia, Botswana, Sudan and Tanzania in Africa; Honduras in America; and New Zealand in the Pacific were of this nature. The same argument holds true for the relations between France and Morocco, Algeria, Tunisia, Senegal, Ghana, Mauritania, Upper Volta and Dahomey; Belgium's relations with Zaire; Portugal's relations with Angola, Mozambique, and Guinea Bissau; and Holland's relations with Indonesia. The establishment of such economic, political, social, cultural, and even religious institutions in colonies, in the service of colonial powers, called for a native staff. This staff consisted of people trained in a Western fashion, brought up to defend and protect the interests of the metropolitan country. In this way they were an extension of the colonialist state inside the colony.

Semi-colonies are societies which have a state founded on a traditional social order and possessing a long history. China, Iran, and the Ottoman Empire were in the position of semi-colonies at one time. In the nineteenth century, faced with the increasing pressure of expanding imperialist states, such countries felt the need to train their own administrative cadres and reorganize their economic, social, political, cultural, and military institutions.

The Political Status of Kurdistan and the Kurdish Nation: A Country and a Nation Without an Identity

Kurdistan is neither a full nor a semi-colony. The political status of the Kurdish nation is far less than the status of a colony. The Kurds are a people the world wants to enslave, render devoid of identity, and wipe off the face of this earth—along with the Kurdish language, culture and history—until every trace of Kurdish identity has been eliminated. Since the first quarter of the twentieth century, the Kurdish people have been engaged in challenging this status, or rather, lack of status, imposed upon them by the imperialist powers and their collaborators in the Middle East, through trying every possible road to freedom including armed struggle.

At this point, it should be mentioned that although a number of states may collaborate with imperialist powers on various issues, such as forming military alliances in the way that Egypt did with the United States in the postwar period, the countries which are collaborating with the imperialist powers towards the annihilation of the Kurdish nation are also occupation forces in the area. Turkey, Iran, Iraq, and Syria, in addition to being collaborators with outside powers, are also occupation forces which have partitioned and annexed Kurdistan.

There is no doubt that, like most colonized regions, Kurdistan's stores of raw materials, its vast natural wealth in petroleum, copper, coal and phosphate, soil, forests, and water are exploited and marketed for industry. However, in the case of Kurdistan, a number of elements not found in classical colonies come into play, reducing Kurdistan's status below that of a colony. We can get a better understanding of this by taking a look, for example, at the relations which formerly existed between Great Britain and Uganda. There is a country known as Uganda, a former British colony, with defined borders. The people living in this country are not British, nor is Uganda considered a part of Great Britain. There was no attempt to transform the native population into Englishmen. When Uganda gained its independence following constitutional negotiations in the late 1960s, its existing borders were not altered. Likewise, the same situation held true for most of the other former colonies of Great Britain, as well as Portugal and France. The people native to the French colonies were not said to be French, nor were there efforts to make them so. Both the French and the native inhabitants were aware of this state of affairs.

The situation in Kurdistan, however, bears no resemblance to the above scenario. In none of the countries where Kurds reside are they considered to be Kurds. In Turkey they are regarded as Turks, in Iran they are considered to be Persians, and in Iraq and Syria they are said to be Arabs. Naturally this means second class "Turks," "Persians," and "Arabs." All of these countries implement harsh assimilation policies and the Kurdish identity is denied with vehemence. The gains achieved through the Kurdish armed struggle in Iran and Iraq are another matter to be dealt with elsewhere.

Following the break up of the Ottoman Empire at the end of World War I, a number of colonial states (mandates) were founded, such as Iraq, Syria, Jordan, Palestine, and Lebanon. However, no Kurdish state was created even as a colony. The Kurdish nation was carved up and distributed among Iraq (which was then a British colony), Syria (which was under French domination), and Turkey, with the intention that the names "Kurd" and "Kurdistan" be erased from all languages and histories forever. The case of Eastern Kurdistan, however, is slightly different; the latter has been under Iranian dominion since the mid seventeenth century.

All Kurdish struggles for independence, freedom, and national rights since the end of World War I have been drowned in blood. The struggles of Sheikh Mahmud Berzenci, and later, those of Molla Mustafa Barzani in Southern Kurdistan; Simko and Qadi Mohammed in Eastern Kurdistan; the struggles in Kochgiri in Northern Kurdistan, and the battles waged under the leadership of Sheikh Said, Ihsan Nuri and Seyid Rıza, have all ended in bloodbaths as a result of the complicity and cooperation between British imperialists and their Middle Eastern collaborators.

Kurdistan's borders have never been clearly defined. The different states colonizing it have made major changes in the natural borders of the region through forced migrations, massacres, genocide, the introduction of immigrants from the Balkans and refugees from Afghanistan, in their efforts to Arabize, Persianize, or Turkify Kurds. Forced emigration of the native Kurdish population and their replacement by Turks, Arabs, and Persians and the establishment of state farms and military garrisons on the most productive lands are just some of the policies enforced by the states which administer Kurdistan. The small section of Kurdistan within the borders of the Republic of Armenia in the Soviet Union should not be overlooked either. Forced emigration has been applied there as well. In 1944 Kurds were forced to leave this republic en masse to Central Asia.

How the Policy of Divide and Rule Facilitates the Colonialists

The policy of divide and rule is of great utility for those states which colonize Kurdistan. This is obvious. When several states have mutual interests in the division of the same country, it is easy for them to enforce a common regime for the protection of those same interests. Claiming rights over parts of the same country does not always cause intervening states to be at odds with each other. They have reason to cooperate to reduce their differences to a minimum in order to maintain their common interests. The continuation of these interests compels such states to maintain good relations.

An imperialist battle was waged over Kurdistan between 1915-1925. Those claiming rights over Kurdish territory were openly engaged in an intensive battle over who would get the bigger share. This period was characterized by conflict and armed confrontations. The decision of the various parties to reach a negotiated settlement led to the division of Kurdistan, and the period following this partition became one of collaboration. The states which have divided Kurdistan know that their common interest lies in strengthening their collaboration.

The policies implemented by Israel with regard to Palestinians when compared to the policies of implemented by Iran, Iraq, Turkey, and Syria towards the Kurds gives us a better understanding of the issues involved. To take one example, the struggles which have taken place between the Palestinians and Israeli security forces since the beginning of 1988 have been given widespread coverage in the Turkish media. Photographs in newspapers and film coverage broadcast on TV have consistently presented the events in full graphic detail. Demonstrations against the policies of the Israeli government, as well as rallies, forums, and panel discussions have been organized by political currents of both the left and right. There is certainly nothing wrong in this, nor in the sensitivity exhibited by the media on this issue. This is not the problem. The problem is the way events going on elsewhere in the Middle East at the same time have been handled. In mid-March 1988, Kurdish peshmergas who were collaborating with the Iranian administration gained control of the town of Halabja in Southern Kurdistan, thereby forcing the colonialist Iraqi administration to abandon the area. While withdrawing, however, the Iraqi army assaulted the town with chemical weapons. According to the reports of international news agencies, the number of Kurds who lost their lives as a result of this chemical attack was approximately 5,000 people, with over 10,000 wounded. Kurdish sources have stated that the true figures were actually much greater. Without any question, this assault, in which thousands of women, children, and elderly people were massacred, can be classified as a genocide. The attitude towards these events by the Turkish government, political parties, universities, writers, the press and media is noteworthy. The same people who had raised such an outcry over the death of a single Palestinian, chose to remain silent and unconcerned in the face of the massacre of over 5,000 Kurds and the wounding of 10,000 more. They pretended to be unaware of what was going on. This double standard is the crux of the issue.

The USA was unable to employ chemical weapons in Vietnam, nor the Soviet Union against Islamic fundamentalists in Afghanistan. As for the Israelis, no matter how great their rage at the Palestinians and the PLO, they did not make use of such weapons. They would not dare take such a step due to the reaction of Arab and Islamic countries, as well as international public opinion. Above all, they would be reluctant to bring on the wrath of the Israeli public itself. It should not be forgotten that Israel is, after all, a democratic country. Saddam Hussein, on the other hand, has been able to employ chemical weapons with relative ease. He knows quite well that in doing so he will meet no criticism from neighboring countries, Turkey, the Arab states, or any other Islamic nation. As far as world public opinion goes, he can just pretend not to notice. It is just this indifference, this failure to react, which enables Saddam Hussein to get away with committing such crimes of genocidal proportions. This is undoubtedly one of the conveniences of the policy of divide and rule. Similarly, the chemical weapons used on both sides during the Iran-Iraq war were directed only against Kurds, who were waging a struggle for national liberation.

The fascist and colonialist Iraqi regime unleashed chemical warfare in Halabja on 17 March 1988. The summit meeting of the Islamic Conference took place in Kuwait on 20 March 1988. The Islamic Conference summit discussed in detail everything from Afghanistan to Palestine and from the Iran-Iraq war to the oppression of the Turkish minority in Bulgaria, passing resolutions on each of these issues. The genocide of the Kurds, however, was not on the agenda, nor was it even brought up for discussion. The Soviet Union was denounced for its presence in Afghanistan and Israel for the terrorist policies applied against Palestinians. Bulgaria was denounced for forcing Turks to change their names and assimilate into the Bulgarian community. It never occurred to any of the Islamic Conference participants, however, to denounce Saddam Hussein's regime for having massacred over 5,000 Kurdish children, women, and elderly people, with over 10,000 more seriously wounded. The issue was not even discussed. This, then, is the primary reason for the ease with which the Saddam Hussein administration was able to carry out such a massacre. He knew he was not going to be called to account for his actions by international, Islamic, and Arab institutions, as such institutions have resolutely opposed the inclusion of Kurdish representatives on their bodies. These international organizations facilitate colonialist states in applying their policies of divide and rule. This is what is meant by Kurdistan as an "interstate colony."

There is a big difference between the way the imperialist European states divided and shared Africa in the late nineteenth century, and the way Kurdistan was divided up earlier by the imperialist powers of Great Britain and France in collaboration with Kemalists and Iran. In 1885, borders were drawn up for nearly 50 African states which are today independent countries. The Kurdish nation, however, with a population of close to 30 million in the Middle East, does not number amongst these states. They still strive, through armed struggle, to protect their identity and reject imperialist, colonialist, and racist settlements being imposed upon them.

Imperialist powers also divided up the Arab nation in the early twentieth century. The latter, however, managed to ensure the establishment of individual states and colonies (mandates), each of which gained independence following constitutional negotiations at the end of World War II. The division of the Arab nation does not resemble the way the Kurdish nation was divided. The same holds true for the divisions of Germany, Korea, and Vietnam, all of which led to the establishment of individual states. Kurdistan was divided up between Iran and the other states which emerged following the break up of the Ottoman Empire. This division facilitated the annihilation of Kurdistan.

The Common Colony of Kurdistan

Deep differences exist between the situation of Palestine and Kurdistan. The Kurds are surrounded by enemies on every side. In fact, Kurds are trying to maintain their existence inside what is practically a hell. Palestine is surrounded by friendly forces, or forces which can be said to be friendly.

They have only one enemy—Israel. As for Israel, it has many enemies, including all 22 Arab states and 42 Islamic states, who, if not enemies, are at least unfriendly. The division of Kurdistan amongst several states has increased their enemies and left them friendless. Although in recent years Kurdistan's friends seem to be increasing, these new friends are far away. The Palestinians are always able to obtain political, financial, and moral support from neighboring Arab countries. When their struggle leaves them in difficult straits they are able to take refuge in one or more of these countries and then continue their struggle both politically and militarily from there. No matter what their relations with Egypt or Jordan, Syria or Lebanon, Iraq, Tunisia, Kuwait, Saudi Arabia, Algeria, and Yemen, this is at least holds true in theory. These states are obliged to aid the Palestinians and the PLO financially, morally, and politically if only to address public opinion in their own countries.

The Kurds forced to flee for their lives from the chemical attacks used against them in Southern Kurdistan and to seek refuge in Northern Kurdistan were locked into camps surrounded by barbed wire fences where they were kept under constant surveillance. They also met with great difficulty entering Turkey in the first place. Since everything possible is done to liquidate the Kurdish movement in Turkey, it is natural for the Turkish government to cooperate with Iraq. The development of a single attitude towards Kurds is emerging as a real situation.

The Palestinian issue appears as an Arab issue, as a result of which other countries wishing to maintain good relations with Arab nations give strong support to Palestinians and the PLO. They feel obliged to do so. The Kurdish issue, on the contrary, appears as an anti-Arab issue. Thus, once again, countries wishing to maintain good relations with Arab nations feel obliged to support the Arab states of Iraq and Syria against the Kurds and turn a deaf ear to the just struggle of Kurds for existence. Due to the oil wealth of Arab countries, other countries consider it important to develop better trade relations, increase exports, win contract bids, and make investments in Arab countries.

Since the Kurdish struggle is also perceived as an anti-Turkish and anti-Persian struggle, what we have said regarding those who wish to maintain good relations with the Arab nations is also true for those who wish to maintain good relations with Turkey and Iran. Such countries pretend to be unaware of the Kurds' just struggle, taking the side of the racist and colonialist governments of Turkey and Iran. The development of trade relations takes precedence over universal values of human rights and the equality of nations. Turkey, Iran, Iraq, and Syria are skilled at using their potential for trade investment as tools for blackmail. They say, "If you draw up any resolutions against us on such and such an issue, we won't give you this contract bid," or "If you refrain from doing such and such against Turkey, we will buy two fleets of aircraft from you," etc.

Therefore, although the Palestinians receive strong support in various international institutions, the Kurds, whose struggle is equally just, are continually left to fend for themselves. The Palestinians began their struggle with Israel in the mid-1960s, and were able shortly thereafter to participate in international institutions such as the United Nations and the Islamic Conference. This was due to their many friends with influential positions in these bodies. Kurdistan has many enemies, and the friends it has avoid getting involved in the just struggle of Kurds on account of the reactions this might incur from its many enemies. This, of course, only holds true for states and the international institutions they support. However, there is more interest from democratic minded public opinion which is continually becoming stronger and more widespread.

It is countries such as the United States of America and the Soviet Union, as well as organizations such as the European Community, which conduct their compromised policies in the way we have outlined above. The first thing they take into consideration is the economic and development potential of 100 million Arabs, not to mention as many Iranians and Turks. The policies of socialist and communist states are not much different. It is totally misleading to give credence to basic principles of socialism, such as the right of nations to self-determination, when looking at the action of these countries. In reality, the policies of the socialist-communist states are not very different from those of the capitalist states. The former are in fact even better at turning a deaf ear when it is in their interest to do so. An example of this is the fact that when chemical weapons were used against the Kurds in Southern Kurdistan, the USA and various other countries in Europe and elsewhere did, in fact, denounce Iraq for its actions, even though rather weakly, while the USSR and the Eastern Block countries did not utter a single word of protest. Sadly, the Palestinian Liberation Organization also chose to remain silent on the matter. This was almost equal to giving one's approval to Saddam Hussein's genocidal crimes, and his fascist and colonialist practices. It is just such responses that give him the courage to continue his policies.

We have given reasons why Israel is unable to use chemical and biological weapons against Palestinians. Let's just imagine, however, what would happen if it did. Demonstrations and mass protests would go on for days, weeks, months, in the Arab states, the Islamic countries, and many other places throughout the world. Panel discussions, conferences, and various forums would be organized denouncing Israel. These would be attended by international institutions. The national parliaments of different countries would pass resolutions and the issue would be placed on the agenda of international bodies. Israel would be isolated. However, when chemical weapons were actually used against Kurds, there were no more than a few feeble murmurs of protest, certainly not enough to dissuade anyone who has such genocidal intentions to carry on as before. This is the result of Kurdistan having been divided and shared out amongst different states. The policy of divide and rule suits those who practice it, and these states are increasing their cooperation in colonizing Kurdistan.

The Kurdish Issue is not a Minority Issue

It should be stressed that the Kurds are not a minority. The Kurds live in Kurdistan, which has always been their homeland and their country. They have not migrated there from any other area, like the Turks, for example, who migrated to Anatolia in the latter half of the eleventh century. Similar to Arabs and Persians, they are native to the Middle East. The difference is that Kurds have been divided up and placed under the domination of others as a result of imperialist and colonialist policies. This makes the Kurds appear as minorities in different states within whose borders they live. Nevertheless 15-20 million people are not a minority. The latter is a different concept altogether.

Recently, certain racist and colonialist Turkish politicians, such as Bülent Ecevit, have come out and said that Kurds are not a minority but, in fact, part of the majority. He said that the Kurds, like the Turks, were instrumental in the founding of the Turkish Republic. This is why the Kurds should not insist on linguistic, cultural, national or democratic rights... For them to claim such rights would be the promotion of separatism and division. Ecevit also claimed that the name Turk, rather than belonging to one ethnic group, actually refers to a new nation formed by the fusion of the Turks, Kurds, Circassians, Arabs and others living within the borders defined by the National Pact of 1920.

Such fraudulent assertions must be vehemently refuted. The recognized minorities in Turkey, such as Armenians, Greeks, and Jews, clearly possess rights the Kurds are denied. How can a majority be denied rights which even minorities enjoy? Turkey denies recognition of the national and democratic rights of Kurds by claiming that "there is no such people known as Kurds, everyone is a Turk." By denying the Kurds' existence and claiming them to be Turks, the Turkish government tries to prove that Kurds have no national rights since they do not exist in the first place. Turkish politicians and intellectuals like Bülent Ecevit deny Kurdish rights by saying they are a majority anyway, which is just another version of the official state ideology. These same persons, however, also react vehemently against Bulgarian journalists, when the latter state that the Turkish minority there has not learned Bulgarian because "the state has been unable to teach them." In this case, Turkish politicians and intellectuals, like Ecevit, protest that learning Turkish is a basic right. Thus they claim that one nation is unworthy of the same basic rights as their own nation.

Turkish politicians and intellectuals such as Bülent Ecevit protest that Western countries maintain double standards when they do not protest sufficiently against the oppression of the Turkish minority in Bulgaria. In doing so, however, the Turkish intellectuals are unable to hide their own double standards. The oppression of the Kurds in Turkey is certainly many times harsher than that the oppression of Turks in Bulgaria. As long as this continues, the West is unlikely to take the wishes of Turkish state intellectuals very seriously, especially since in recent years western democratic circles have started to take a closer interest in the Kurdish issue.

The Kurdish issue is not a question of minority rights. The heart of the matter lies in the fact that the Kurdish nation has been split up and divided, and their right to establish an independent state has been usurped by imperialist powers and their Middle Eastern collaborators.

Kurdistan and the Liquidation of the Classic Colonies

There is also another vital difference between Kurdistan and classical colonialism. When the status of the colonial world was being redefined under the auspices of the League of Nations following World War I, this was not intended to be a permanent solution. The intention was that, once the colonialist nations had strengthened the economic, political, and administrative structures of their colonies, they would withdraw and the latter would be granted independence. Meanwhile, the native population would be "civilized." In Africa, for instance, the number of nations to achieve independence as a result of armed struggle is few. Most of these countries became independent following negotiations over the new country's constitution. The division of Kurdistan, however, was intended as a permanent solution. The Kurds were to be divided up, enslaved, deprived of identity, and isolated from one another for eternity. In this way, Kurdistan was afforded a status lower than that of a colony. Its collective identity is nonexistent.

Let's take a look at the nineteenth century and the causes which gave rise to colonialism. First of all, the countries where industrialization was underway had a need for raw materials, many of which were only available from the Middle and Far East, Central and South America, or Africa. Likewise, these same regions from which raw materials could be obtained were seen as potential markets for the new products of the industrialized nations. Competition began amongst the latter for control of the former. The industrializing nations hastened to send technicians, administrators, merchants, educators, men of religion, and security forces where they wanted to establish their control. Later they would increase these security forces under the pretext of needing to protect their own settlers against the "threat" posed by the natives.

In addition to the above, certain regions were also colonized or taken under the direct control of imperialist states on account of strategic interests. The USA intervention in Vietnam, for instance, falls into this category. Whoever controlled Vietnam had access to the entire Far East. It was also thought that the loss of this control would lead to reduced influence in the region. In terms of the foreign policy of the United States, this is known as the domino theory. Should any country of Southeast Asia fall into communist hands as a result of a revolutionary movement, other countries in the region would sooner or later follow course, which would mean a great blow to United States foreign policy in all of Southeast Asia.

The above-mentioned model can also be observed in the colonization of Kurdistan. Kurdistan's wealth in petroleum, water, copper, iron, phosphate, coal and other natural resources was a significant element in the region's colonization. Today, however, the determining factor is the division of Kurdistan, the enforcement of colonialist policies there by several states, and the strategic interests that reinforce this order.

There is more than a mere quantitative difference between a nation being colonized by one, and a nation colonized by more than one, state. The colonization of Kurdistan by four states creates a different context in colony-colonialist relationships. This is what we mean when we point out that Kurdistan is not even a colony.

Nor should Kurdistan's division into four sections be confused with the policy known as "Balkanization." The latter is another form of divide and rule where hostility is fomented between different people as a way to introduce political instability in areas where different people live. The division of Kurdistan is a process that is completely contrary to this. The states which colonize Kurdistan cooperate with one another in order to maintain their interests. When a conflict erupts between Kurdish national forces and these colonial states, it gives rise to instability, but this instability occurs in spite of the desires of the colonialist states.

The Imperialist Struggle to Divide Kurdistan 1915-1925

One of the most important aspects of the 1923 Lausanne Treaty was the imperialist division of Kurdistan. For the Turks, the treaty of Lausanne represents the founding of an independent Turkish state and the guarantee by international treaty. However, for the Kurds, this same treaty represents the institutionalization of their servitude and colonization. The approach to history from a class struggle perspective, to the exclusion of the wishes and will of ethnic groups, leads to a faulty analysis. For instance, Turks and Greeks have very different views concerning the Turko-Greek war of 1919-1923. Arabs and Turks have great differences of opinion over the situation of the Ottoman Empire during World War I. The same is true for Armenians and Turks, and Iranians and Iraqis during the Iran-Iraq war. Turkish universities and writers will always interpret this treaty from their own perspective, which means using it to justify the continuation of the status quo, as they have done so up until now. These Turkish writers are also the ones who have written that Kurds are Turks. The Kurds must research and write their own history, as other peoples do. And I must stress the importance of approaching issues from the point of view of ethnic groups. Turkish Marxists claim that they address issues from a class standpoint but they do so as "Turkish Marxists." A class viewpoint should not mean that Kurdish identity is neglected.

For a nation to be subjected to a policy of partition and foreign rule is one of the greatest catastrophes which can befall it. Such a policy scatters the brain and smashes the backbone so that the victim nation faces great obstacles in pulling itself back together again. The Kurds experienced such a blow in the first half of the seventeenth century, and their situation became even more critical in their division during the early twentieth century. For over seventy years they have been fighting to overcome the damage inflicted upon them and striving to let people know of the injustice which they have met. A similar division lies at the root of the Armenian issue. The Armenians were split between Iran and the Ottoman Empire, then the Ottoman Empire, Tsarist Russia, and Iran.

The struggles between the Kemalist and the British in the 1920s during the Turko-Greek and Turko-Armenian wars was essentially over who would get a bigger share of Kurdistan. There was essentially nothing anti-imperialist about it.

Several important events should be highlighted in the history of Kurdistan. As far back as 3100 B.C. reference is made to the "Gutis," a people native to Mesopotamia. One of the more important events of antiquity was the Assyrian invasion and conquest of Kurdistan, which is referred to in an ancient inscription, "The entire land of the Gutis from Mount Ararat to Harran was painted in blood." The reign of the Assyrians was ended by the Medes around 600 B.C.

The seventh century marks the date of the Kurds' conversion to Islam. History tells us that the Kurds experienced their first bloody encounter with the armies of Islam during the time of Caliph Omar in 640 A.D. The social, political, and economic order of the Kurds up till this date still needs to be researched. What means of production did they possess and what techniques of production did they use? What did they sow and reap, and how? What were their religious beliefs prior to their conversion to Islam? How did their conversion alter the preexisting social and political institutions? All of the above are important topics in Kurdish history and need to be researched.

The eleventh century, when the Kurds first met up with the Oghuz Turks migrating from Central Asia is another significant date in Kurdish history. Once again, how did this encounter take place, and what effects did it have on existing Kurdish social and political institutions?

In the thirteenth and fourteenth centuries the Kurds were subjected to raids by the Mongols and Timurlane. Later, in the early sixteenth century, a major portion of Kurdistan was incorporated into the Ottoman Empire. In 1514, following an important battle at Chaldiran between the Persian and Ottoman Empires, a major section of Kurdistan came under the rule of the Ottoman Sultan Selim I (the Grim).

In the mid-seventeenth century Kurdistan was split between the Ottoman Empire and Iran, initiating a process through which, with time, Kurdistan was divided into more and more pieces. What were the causes leading to the nation's partition, and how did this facilitate the Ottoman and Persian Empires? What weaknesses of the Kurds were exploited by their enemies in order to divide and rule Kurdistan at that time?

In the early nineteenth century the Iranian portion of Kurdistan was further divided following battles between Iran and Tsarist Russia. A section of Northwest Kurdistan was then incorporated into the Tsarist

Empire. Conflict between the Kurds and the Ottoman Empire continued all through the nineteenth century.

Although the events we have briefly mentioned are of no minor significance, it is primarily the events which have taken place after World War I which have determined the situation as it exists today. 1915 to 1925 was the period of the imperialist struggle which brought on the division of Kurdistan. Any attempt to justify this division with the argument that "the Kurds never possessed an independent state up until that time anyway" is false. It should not be forgotten that the European colonies established in Africa were imposed on traditional societies which had not yet reached the stage of founding their own states. Borders were virtually drawn with rulers. What were the causes which allowed Kurdistan to be the object of harsh imperialist policies? Who were the original instigators of these policies? Which states have benefited by the practice of divide and rule in Kurdistan? Why is it that Kurdistan, rather than Iraq, Jordan, or Syria was divided up to be shared as a colony of two newly established colonial states (Iraq, Syria) and two older states (Turkey and Iran)? What were the weaknesses of Kurdish society which rendered it the target of a policy of divide and rule?

Let's take a look at the first quarter of the twentieth century. The Ottoman empire was on the verge of breaking up, and the various people under its rule—Arabs, Albanians, Bulgarians, Armenians, Kurds etc.—embarked on a struggle for self-determination. The British and French imperialists had major interests in the region, as did the Germans and Italians. Tsarist Russia also had a role in this conflict of interests. The 1917 Bolshevik Revolution turned the world upside down. The relationship between all these conflicting elements needs to be investigated and backed up with facts to fully grasp the situation in which Kurds found themselves at this time. It is not sufficient to talk about the relationship between the Nationalist Forces and the British and French or the Bolsheviks. One must go further and examine the relationship between Great Britain and the Bolsheviks as well, and what the effects of this relationship were on the regional balance of power.

In Turkey, the word Kurd is not used in official statements, the press, amongst writers, or in politics. Instead the word "divisive forces" is usually used. This is an effort to mask the official policy of "divide, rule and destroy" from people's consciousness. The Kurds are not divisive, it is they who have been divided. The real divisive forces are British imperialists, French imperialists, Kemalists, the Shah of Iran, as well as the Arabs who collaborated with them.

Statements made by government officials and politicians in ceremonial speeches in Turkey that foreign powers "wanted to break up Turkey and wipe the Turkish nation off the face of the earth and from all history... that they wanted to enslave the Turkish nation who had lived free and independent for centuries" are also intended to conceal the policy of "divide, rule and destroy" which is being enforced on the Kurds today. Such declarations are intended to prevent people from becoming aware of the truth behind these policies.

The oft repeated motto "the indivisibility of the country and its people" is intended to serve the same purpose. By referring to the indivisibility of the Turkish nation, they are implying that the Kurdish nation is to remain divided in eternity. The Ottoman Empire, which was composed of numerous nations such as the Turks, Arabs, Greeks, Armenians, Serbs, Croatians, Romanians, Bulgarians, Kurds, Circassians, Laz et al., was said to be a "cosmopolitan empire." How is it then, that the Republic of Turkey, which comprises of at least two, if not more of these nations, is referred to as a "national" state?

Subsequent to World War I and the break up of the Ottoman Empire during the Turco-Greek and Turco-Armenian wars, the battles between Turks and Kurds at Kochgiri, and the battles between Kurds and British forces in southern Kurdistan, led to the partition of Kurdistan. As a result of this process, Turkey, Iran, Britain (Iraq) and France (Syria) each came into possession of a section of Kurdistan. This period also requires serious research and detailed documentation. However, this is not the aim of this work. As stated earlier, the aim of this work is to draw attention to certain issue and raise pertinent questions.

The Focal Point of the Kurdish Issue: The Division of Kurdistan and the Application of the Policy of "Divide, Rule and Exterminate" on the Kurdish Nation

Although the policy of "divide and rule" in Kurdistan was the result of a wider imperialist intervention in this region, the policy "divide, rule and destroy" was devised by regional collaborators. Imperialism does not exterminate the peoples living in the territories it occupies, nor does it liquidate their culture. Its primary objective is to increase the area under its control and create new markets for its products. In some cases, imperialist powers have even expanded cultural activities in their colonies. The British, for instance, opened schools in Iraq where Kurdish was the language of instruction, while the French in Syria published books and periodicals in the Kurdish language. They made no efforts to restrict the development of the Kurdish language and literature. Moreover, it was not the great imperialist powers who sought to physically exterminate Kurds through the use of chemical weapons. This was also a policy of regional collaborators.

In a speech made to the Turkish Historical Society in the 1930s, Mustafa Kemal made his ideas known on the national liberation struggles waged by the Balkan nations against the Ottoman Empire. In answer to a question he himself posed, he pointed out that extensive research on the Balkan peoples carried out by Slavic research institutions indicated that these nations revolted against the Ottoman Empire after attaining national consciousness.[1]

Two major conclusions could be reached from the above statements. One was the need for nations wishing to live freely to stand up for their own history, language, culture, literature, and art just as the Turks did following the founding of the Republic. The other was that if a power wanted to enslave and colonize a people, then it should deprive its victims of an alphabet, outlaw their language and culture, and take all possible measures to prevent the development of the latter attributes. This was because once a colonized people attained national consciousness and the desire to live their own lives, they would revolt against their masters. A people prevented from speaking their own language and made unaware of the very prohibition against them would remain an unconscious and enslaved nation. A people living under such conditions would be wide open to unrestrained political and economic exploitation.

The psychological dimensions of the prohibition of one's language can be expressed as follows. People prohibited from speaking their own language are like people whose tongue has been cut off. This leads to the loss of social, psychological, as well as physical integrity. The result is a people who are unhealthy, unbalanced, and lack confidence. A society composed of such persons is an unhealthy society, easily ruled by others. Anything can be imposed on such a society through orders, beatings, and threats. They can be channeled in any direction. The only way for such a society to recuperate its health is for it to become aware of the prohibitions against it and to examine its own identity. There is no greater factor in shaking off the colonial order than the development and growth of this process of consciousness.

The banning of the Kurdish language, the obstacles placed on the study of the Kurdish language, culture, and literature, the prohibitions on research into Kurdish history, and the general repression of Kurds should be evaluated from this perspective. Everything possible must be done to prevent Kurds from reaching a nationalist awareness. Nothing must remain of the Kurdish language, literature, culture, history and lifestyle.

The process of breaking up Kurdistan has made the four states which have partitioned it utterly dependent on wider imperialist interests. This is because these local governments are dependent on imperialist aid to maintain the repression against periodic Kurdish revolts. Since the first quarter of this century, all rebellions which have taken place in Southern and Eastern Kurdistan were repressed with the assistance of the British. It is utterly misleading to think that the British aided the Kurds in the Sheikh Said rebellion. At that time Britain was engaged in a bloody battle against the Kurds in Southern Kurdistan. Moreover, the Turkish army, which traveled to Diyarbekir from Ankara to repress the rebellion, even passed through Syria by railroad. It should not be forgotten that Syria was a French colony at the time. If France had not allowed the Turkish army to travel through their territory, events might have turned out differently.

Major battles between the various imperialist forces, as well as these imperialist forces and their regional collaborators, were waged over the partition of Kurdistan. With the establishment of an international system of colonization, these conflicts turned to concessions, and then collaboration. This collaboration was then institutionalized into an international colonial system.

The Slogans of Kemalism

Although Kemalists were close collaborators with imperialist states in the breakup of Kurdistan, they never lost the opportunity to say, "We were the first to wage a struggle of national liberation against imperialism and colonialism. We led the way for the exploited and colonized peoples of the East. We inspired them to wage the struggle for national liberation..." Kemalists never want to be reminded of the fact of the Kurds, and they consciously avoid any discussion of the issue. They do not hesitate to turn you over to the police and ensure your imprisonment to shut you up should you dare bring up this issue. They speak everywhere, and at all times, and always give only one side of the picture—on TV, radio, newspapers, educational institutions, the barracks, and the mosques... A study of the contradictions between what Mustafa Kemal said and wrote in the 1920s, and what really happened, would without doubt make interesting reading.

Another method employed by the Kemalists to conceal the racist and colonialist policies practice on Kurds is to accuse the Kurds themselves of being racist. The prohibition of the Kurdish language and culture, the employment of all possible means to force Kurds to speak Turkish and adopt Turkish identities, the forced changes to the names of individuals and villages, the imposition of fines on all who speak Kurdish, the removal of all traces of Kurdish language and culture... are all, according to Kemalists, revolutionary and democratic steps. For the Kurds, however, to demand their own national rights, or to organize for this reason, is racist and chauvinist. Moreover, when the Turks in Bulgaria do just this, they are praised as progressive people revolting against racist, colonialist, fascist, and inhuman practices.

Human Rights and the Kurds

The Kurds in Turkey are only able to benefit from equality and civil rights to the extent that they renounce their national character and their true identity. Equality, the basic principle of democracy, human rights, as well as economic and social rights, are contingent upon the denial of their true identity as Kurds. This policy is prescribed in the police stations and prisons throughout Turkey. It is stated over and over through tyranny, persecution, and torture. It is announced time and again through court indictments and resolutions. The press, media, and state bureaucracy are employed to ensure this as the predominant way of thinking. The same holds for the educational institutions, religion, and so on.

A person who denies his true identity as a Kurd to become a Turk, one who says, “I’m a Turk, I’m happy,” can be everything—a worker, doorman, student, teacher, athlete, businessman, military officer, general, minister, professor, or anything. However, one who chooses to remain a Kurd and defends Kurdish national rights cannot be anything in Turkey except indicted and condemned.

In the early years of the Turkish Republic, great care was taken by government officials to emphasize this perspective. The Republican People’s Party General Vice-Chairman and Prime Minister İsmet İnönü said, “The only nation in this country with the right to demand ethnic and religious rights are the Turks. No one else possesses this right.”[2] Similarly, Turkey’s Minister of Justice, Mahmut Esat Bozkurt, also put it in no uncertain terms, when he said, “The only master, the sole lord in this country is the Turk. Those not of Turkish descent have only one right in this country—the right to be servants or slaves. All friends and foes, even the mountains, are to know this truth."[3] For Bozkurt, those who were not Turks—Kurds in other words—were only permitted to be "servants" or "slaves." But even a slave or servant is something. One can say "Kurdish servant" or "Kurdish slave." As a Kurd, however, one had no right to be even that. One could only be accused, condemned, and imprisoned as a Kurd. This is the point that I am trying to get across.

In early 1923, at the Lausanne Conference, the situation was very different. In his memoirs, İsmet İnönü tells us how Kurds fought with heart and soul in the national struggle for independence, how they exhibited the greatest ardor protecting the homeland from the Armenian threat, and how they fought side by side with the Turks. As he put it, "In our speeches in Lausanne, we defended as one nation and won the acceptance of our national claims by saying, 'We Turks and Kurds.'"[4]

İsmet İnönü says that the Treaty of Lausanne was achieved by the concept of "We Turks and Kurds," that it was this understanding which enabled the Turkish leadership to have their national claims accepted by the West. Once the Republic was founded, however, he himself strove towards the development of the denial of Kurdish existence as one of the new state's basic tenets.

Prime Minister Turgut Özal has stated in various speeches that no discrimination is made between Turks and Kurds, that there are many Kurdish military officers, generals, members of parliament, ministers, professors, governors, judges, and so forth. In a speech made to the European Council Parliamentary Assembly on 27 September 1989, he made statements to this effect.[5] The persons to whom he was referring, however, certainly did not reach these positions as Kurds! They reached them by becoming Turks, by denying their true identities, their Kurdishness. Take MPs, for example, once elected, how are they sworn into office? Do they not declare how they are inspired by Turkish patriotism, and take an oath to safeguard it? Is it possible to attain such a position in Turkey as a Kurd and defender of Kurdish national rights?

Double Standards Applied in Interpreting the Principle of Equality

For equality, human rights and civil liberties, as well as economic and social rights, to be conditional upon the denial of one's true identity is racism. It is an attitude which underpins genocide. Such a perspective reduces Kurdistan's status to even lower than a colony. Such a policy is a hundred percent violation of international laws for the protection and improvement of human rights, the concepts of law and justice, the United Nations Universal Declaration on Human Rights, and the Helsinki Final Accords. Even when interpreted by Turkish politicians, the Turkish press, and Turkish universities, the assimilationist and genocidal dimensions of these views are clear.

The phrase "Everyone in Turkey is equal; everyone receives the same treatment regardless of language or race," is repeated by state officials and politicians, the press, writers and the universities.[6] Their supposed interpretation of these principles is based on double standards. When they say, "Everyone in Turkey is equal in respect to religious belief; there is no discrimination against persons adhering to different religions or denominations" they mean that just as the Muslims in Turkey are free to worship, so are the Christians. The Greeks and Armenians have churches and the Jews synagogues. Everyone is free to worship. The model of no discrimination on the basis of religion is used to stress that there are various religions and denominations in Turkey, and that these communities are equal.

The phrase, "Everyone in Turkey is equal; there is no discrimination on the basis of language or race," is not, however, interpreted in the same way. What is being said is "Everyone in Turkey is a Turk; all Turks are treated equally. There is no discrimination on the basis of language." Here, the differences and variety of languages are not pointed out; what is being stressed is that everyone in Turkey is a Turk, all Turks are equal, and Turkish is spoken. This shows that equality is contingent upon being a Turk. What should be said, however, is that everyone is equal in respect to language, and that the rights accorded to Turkish also belong to, for example, Kurdish. Only in this way would equality be ensured. But this is not the case.

It is said that everyone who accepts being a Turk is a Turk. At first glance, this may seem to indicate tolerance. One may think that those who do not accept being Turks, who say, for instance, that they are Kurds, are tolerated. Nothing could be further from the truth. There is no such tolerance. According to the official state ideology, everyone is obliged to be a Turk. Being a Kurd is against the law. In Diyarbekir Military Prison alone over forty Kurdish revolutionists were tortured to death between 1981 and 1984 for refusing to say, "I am a Turk and I am happy," and being determined to maintain their Kurdish identities. These revolutionaries paid the price of sending a message to the outside world with their lives. These same persons expressed their protests against state terrorism by putting an end to their lives. Moreover, the actual number of persons to have done so is far more than forty.

The Slogans of Unity and Togetherness

One of the most frequently employed slogans in Turkey is the idea of unity and fellowship. State and government officials and political party leaders say, "Turks and Kurds are brothers, they are an inseparable whole. Just as nails are inseparable from flesh, so Turks and Kurds are an indivisible whole. We have lived on this land together for one thousand years. We share the same religion. We are brothers in faith. We are Muslims. We make no distinction between us. We rule the country together."

The state itself does not say this officially. It makes use of its mouthpieces, such as local politicians and the press. Practically every political body, apart from the CHP-SHP tradition, including the MHP, makes reference to Turkish-Kurdish fraternity. This makes one wonder how this "indivisible whole" happened to be split asunder during the 1920s. How about in the seventeenth century? How is it that today, Iran, Iraq, Turkey, and Syria all covet different parts of Kurdistan? What made the Kemalists collaborate with British and French imperialists in making the Kurds a target for a policy of divide and rule? Certainly none of these facts points to the existence of any "indivisible whole!" This slogan is only an attempt to conceal the tyranny, oppression, violence, and state terrorism to which Kurds have been subjected.

It is said that, "we are one in worry, sorrow, joy, and gladness." "We fought together against the Greeks in Cyprus, making no distinctions between us." The facts, however, refute every one of these falsehoods. Let's take a look back at the events which took place in Halabja in Southern Kurdistan in mid-March, 1988. Over 5,000 Kurds, most of them women, children or elderly people, were killed with chemical weapons by the racist and colonialist Iraqi administration. Did the Turkish government and state authorities exhibit any reaction to this act of genocide? What about Kenan Evren, the President of the Turkish Republic, who was participating in the Islamic Conference summit in Kuwait at the time? Did he place the matter on the agenda for discussion? Is this what is meant to be one in worry and sorrow? On the contrary, just two weeks after these events, the Prime Minister of Turkey, Turgut Özal, visited Baghdad. This was practically like congratulating the Iraqi colonialists for their actions. Turkey has not shown the Kurds in Southern Kurdistan even a tiny fraction of the interest it has shown Palestinians in the latter's struggle. On the contrary, with the air raids the Turkish air force carries out from time to time, the Turkish government reverses any gains Kurds may have made in their struggle in Southern Kurdistan. There is absolutely no comparison between the interest exhibited towards the problems of Turkish Cypriots and Turks in Western Thrace or Bulgaria on the one hand, and Kurds on the other. The Turkish government is continually seeking ways to force Kurds to emigrate and assimilate, including the settlement of Turks from Afghanistan on the most fertile lands in Kurdistan. In spite of all the above, as they implement such policies, the Turkish government still insists that "we are one in worry and sorrow, joy and gladness." Nothing could be more hollow and misleading. Every gain against the Iraqi administration won by Kurds in Southern Kurdistan is greeted with joy and enthusiasm by the people of Northern Kurdistan. These same gains, however, cause Turkish officials and administrators to be overwhelmed with anxiety. Furthermore, to render these gains invalid and prevent further successes, the Turkish air force carries out frequent air raids in Southern Kurdistan under the pretext of "chasing away bandits." The Turkish government collaborates with the Iraqi colonialist regime to prevent any successes by Kurds.

The positions taken by the Turkish daily press, political parties, trade unions, universities, writers, etc., are more or less the same. None of them spoke out against the massacre at Halabja although they were all brimming with enthusiasm over the Turks coming from Bulgaria. We can see how meaningless and misleading is the phrase "we are one in worry, sorrow, joy and gladness." Saying "we fought together against the Greeks in Cyprus, making no distinction between us" is nothing but the barest hypocrisy. The Kurds were sent off to war in the service of Turkish racist and colonialist ambitions. Kurds certainly had nothing to gain or lose from the Greeks, nor was there any conflict existing between them. It was not the Greeks who occupied and colonized Kurdistan. The same is the case when it is said that Kurds fought alongside Turks against Greeks in the West, and Armenians in the South and the East after the World War I period. They tell us, "We fought together against the common enemy and protected the homeland." Who is this common enemy? Why should the Greeks and Armenians be the Kurds' enemies? What did the Kurds gain from these "wars against the common enemy?"

These slogans are nothing but thinly concealed attempts to cover up two-faced, hypocritical, racist policies.

We all know with what warmth and enthusiasm the Turks forced to leave Bulgaria were welcomed in Turkey. A great fanfare was raised over these "race brothers" and "fellow Turks." When Kurds were forced to evacuate Southern Kurdistan after assaults against them by chemical and biological weapons, they were penned up at the border for ages, and many were handed over to the Iraqi government which immediately executed them. Later the press was full of statements like "those coming from Northern Iraq have put a great strain on the budget... those coming from Iraq have become a lot of trouble for us... the peshmergas should leave as soon as possible." Such complaints started as soon as the Kurds arrived. As for the Kurds who had already come, they were all—children and elderly, young and old—herded into camps surrounded by barbed wire. Great efforts were made to ensure that their basic needs were not met. All interest in their welfare as well as material aid of every sort was prohibited. The refugees from Southern Kurdistan were treated as captives and prisoners. Police stations were set up at camp entrances. All possible measures were taken to ensure that they had no contact with anyone other than officially designated authorities.

Turkish governmental authorities went on and on for months trying to convince the West that they should assume part of the expenses for the upkeep of some forty or fifty thousand Kurds. When it came to the Turks fleeing Bulgaria, however, they simply claimed that "even if two million of our race-brothers come, we would gladly accept them. Turkey is a great and wealthy country."

The Turkish government also did all it could to help those coming from Bulgaria, who had relatives here, to contact and stay with their relatives. However, Kurds who also had relatives in Northern Kurdistan, were prevented from establishing any contact with the latter. After all this, who is going to believe the lies about Turks and Kurds being "one in worry and sorrow, joy and gladness?" Yet, anyone who dares speak out and criticize these words is regarded as guilty of committing an offense.

A person who denies his Kurdish identity is allowed to take part in every sort of political, administrative, cultural, and economic activity. There are no barriers against the assumption of duties in the public bureaucracy or elsewhere. A person who chooses to remain a Kurd, defend Kurdish identity, as well as Kurdish national and democratic rights, can never be anything in Turkey other than accused and condemned as a prisoner of the state. Kurds have every right to carry out research on Turkish language and culture; they are even encouraged to do so. If the same Kurds, however, undertake to prepare a Kurdish dictionary, or any sort of research on Kurdish culture, they are faced with long prison sentences. They can protest the oppression of the Turks in Western Thrace and Bulgaria as loudly as they like, but woe to those who dare speak out against the oppression of Kurds. This is why we say that the right to assume duty in the political, diplomatic, or cultural life of Turkey is contingent upon one becoming a Turk. Kurds who love the language, culture, land, and history of their Turkish, Arab, and Persian masters, are praised as "good citizens, good persons." Kurds who stand up for their native language and Kurdistan are charged with being "bandits," "brigands," "traitors," or "cowards."

But, in spite of the threats of harsh sanctions, Kurds have begun to participate in the political and cultural life of Turkey as Kurds, as defenders of Kurdish national and democratic rights. This is gradually becoming more widespread and there is every indication that it will continue to do so.

However, there remain persons born of Kurdish parents who deny their Kurdish identity. They show more grief over a Bulgarian Turk with a nosebleed than over the torture and death of over forty Kurds in Diyarbekir prison for refusing to say they are Turks. If you mention the latter event to them, they will tell you it's none of their business. These same people display absolutely no interest in the massacre of over 5,000 Kurds by chemical weapons. The colonialists exploit the weaknesses of such persons to the maximum. These Kurds are even sent to international institutions to relate the problems of Turks in Cyprus, Bulgaria, and Western Thrace. This is one of the tragedies of our age.

The Problem of Identity Amongst Kurdish Intellectuals

Turkish writers are always proud to emphasize that they are Turks, whether they are addressing a national or international audience. Does the same hold true for Kurdish writers? What about Kurdish journalists, singers, actors, and actresses?

The United Nations and the Kurds

The Kurdish question is one of the most vexing issues facing the United Nations today. The United Nations played a major role in the elimination of colonialism in the post war period by taking the side of the colonies against imperialist powers such as Great Britain, France, Belgium, Holland, Portugal and Spain. However, because of the breakup of Kurdistan, the Kurdish issue has never been on the agenda of the United

Nations, nor of the League of Nations that preceded it. The various governments responsible for Kurdistan's division have resolutely blocked the issue from being discussed. The relations which developed between Iraq and the USSR in the 1960s had no effect on the state of affairs in Southern Kurdistan. In fact, the tyranny, massacre, genocide, and exile carried out by the Baath regime under Saddam Hussein increased from year to year, with the Kurds unable to make their voices heard beyond the wall of steel raised around them.

In February 1963, a coup d'etat by the Baathists in Iraq overthrew the regime of Abdulkerim Kasim. Following the coup, there was a repression of the leaders and members of the Iraqi Communist Party, as were Kurds. Thousands of Communists were tortured and executed. Only those able to make their way to Kurdistan were able to escape with their lives. At this time the USSR brought the Kurdish issues to the U.N. to threaten the interests of Iraq. In fact, it was not the USSR which brought up the subject directly; it was Mongolia at the request of the USSR. In late 1963, another coup d'etat in Iraq ousted the Baathists from power. Gradually the new government began to establish better relations with the Communists and the USSR. The latter then withdrew their proposals from the U.N. and the issue was closed.

Following World War I, the League of Nations took up the search for a homeland for Jews. Following World War II, the United Nations played a major role in the establishment of a Jewish state in Palestine. Neither of these two institutions, however, ever gave the slightest thought for a solution for the Kurdish question. On the contrary, they both approved and encouraged the division of the Kurdish nation and homeland.

The fact that the U.N. passes resolutions against the racist practices in South Africa but turns a deaf ear to the racist practices to which Kurds are subjected should tell us something. Of course the racist practices differ in the two regions. In South Africa public services are separated according to race, and black communities receive services of a very low standard. In Turkey, on the other hand, Kurds are only able to benefit from public services when they deny their identities. The denial of one's identity, and the forced adoption of the identity of an oppressor nation, is a much harsher form of racism.

From time to time the Kurdish issue is compared to the Turkish minority in Bulgaria. Such a comparison is totally misleading. The two issues are totally different due to the simple but crucial fact that there is no Kurdish state anywhere, while Turks living in Cyprus, Bulgaria, and Western Thrace can always rely on the Turkish State to back them up and bring their issue onto the agenda of international institutions—even going to war to defend their interests if necessary. Who is going to bring up the Kurds' problems? The system of international colonization set up in Kurdistan was established for just that reason—to prevent Kurds from establishing a state. This makes it so much easier for others to exploit Kurdish natural resources. Without a state, Kurds have no way of making their voices heard, no one to stand up for them. In recent years some democratic groups and institutions around the world have attempted to address the Kurdish issue.

Let's take a look back at September 1988, when tens of thousands of Kurds were forced to leave Southern Kurdistan and seek refuge in Northern Kurdistan after they were attacked with chemical weapons. The United Nations decided to send a delegation of experts into the region to examine their case. When Iraq refused to permit them entrance to the country, the delegation requested permission to examine the refugees who had entered Turkey. Once again the permission was denied. Nevertheless, this same Turkish government was very insistent on a U.N. team of experts going to Bulgaria less than a year later to examine claims that Turks in that country were being inoculated with unknown vaccines. In both cases the Turkish government made use of its privileges as an independent state. This is another reason for the United Nations to take an interest in the international colonial system applied in Kurdistan.

Turkish authorities and the media were most insistent on the need for Turks coming from Bulgaria to be given the best possible treatment, otherwise Bulgaria would make anti-Turkish propaganda. Why was it then, that the same authorities had no such apprehensions when it came to the mistreatment of Kurdish refugees from the South? Obviously because they knew no other government was going to criticize them regardless of what they did. Should Turkey not be made to consider the possibility that they could be criticized by institutions such as the U.N. for their repeated bad treatment of Kurds?

Amongst the numerous instances of maltreatment was an attempt to poison Kurdish refugees en masse. One example was the poisoning of over 500 Kurds in the Kiziltepe refugee camp in mid-June 1989. No matter how vehemently it is denied by the Turkish authorities and press, facts have been established that as a result of joint efforts by Turkish and Iraqi secret services, certain chemicals were injected into the bread served to camp residents.[7] Iraq continues its racist and colonialist policies against

Kurds in a most conscious and resolute fashion. Shouldn't this be a matter of interest to the United Nations?

Kurdistan is no Longer What it Used to be: the Rise of National Consciousness

Many things are undergoing change in our day, and Kurdistan is amongst them. All parts of Kurdistan are experiencing a process of intense politicization. Especially since 1980, Kurds have been more and more searching and investigating their identity and past. State terrorism and an inflexible state ideology can no longer hold back a society undergoing change as rapidly as the Kurds. Kurdistan is no longer what it used to be. The Kurds are no longer a blind force held back by the terrorist tactics of the army and police, or legends of the greatness of the Turkish nation. Our day is witness to the awakening of the Kurdish masses and the rise of a Kurdish national consciousness. This national consciousness brings along with it political, social, and economic consciousness. The consciousness of Kurds is now in the process of liberation from confusion and primitiveness.

The Turkish left and intellectuals are also being influenced by these changes in Kurdistan. The influence of the official state ideology is now being broken. These changes are the result of years of debate and struggle; they have by no means come about overnight. The countless rebellions which have taken place throughout history, going back to the days of the Ottoman empire, have been of no little significance. The national liberation struggles led under Sheikh Mahmud Berzenci and later Molla Mustafa Barzani in Southern Kurdistan, and the uprising led by Simko in Eastern Kurdistan, the Kurdish Republic of Mahabad, and the uprisings of Sheikh Said, Kochgiri, Ararat, and Dersim have all been factors contributing to this accumulation of national awareness. We are presented with more examples when we look back at the last thirty years in Northern Kurdistan, among which in included the arrest of 49 intellectuals in 1959, and the arrest of 23 intellectuals in 1963. Nor should one forget the events of 1943, the execution of 43 persons, the events surrounding General Mustafa Muglalı. The founding of the Democratic Party of Kurdistan in 1965 marks an important turning point, as does the establishment of the Revolutionary Cultural Associations of the East in 1968.

The publication of the periodicals *Ileri Yurt* (Forward Country) in Diyarbekir in 1958; *Silvan'ın Sesi* (The Voice of Silvan) in Silvan in 1962; *Dicle-Fırat* (Tigris-Euphrates) in Istanbul in 1962; *Deng* (Voice) and *Roja*

Newe in Istanbul in 1963; and *Yeni Akış* (New Current) in Ankara in 1966, and the investigations, arrests, and trials which unfolded around them played a significant role in the development of Kurdish national consciousness. The bulletins put out by the Revolutionary Cultural Associations of the East were also a significant contribution.

At this point we should not overlook the newspaper *Sheresiyar*, which came out in 1970 in Doğu Beyazit. The paper's name led Professor Doctor Hifzi Veldet Velidedeoğlu to write a series of articles which were published in the nationwide daily paper *Cumhurriyet*, denouncing those who put out *Sheresiyar* by claiming that such a name constituted separatist propaganda. According to him, the use of a non-Turkish name constituted treason.[8]

Professor Velidedeoğlu charged the revolutionary and democratic persons struggling against the aghas (feudal landlords) and for democracy and socialism with treason. It was sufficient that the paper's name was Kurdish. For such a person, who was known as a revolutionary and democrat, to denounce Kurdish revolutionists and democrats is not easily understandable. The truth is that it was the cases opened against these publications and their writers, as well as the articles written to denounce them, which were of greater service in the development of Kurdish national consciousness than the contents of the publications themselves. The Kurdish issue showed clearly where the boundaries of Turkish democracy lay, as well as just how far the democratic conscience of Turkish intellectuals would go. All of these contradictions served to widen the views and horizons of Kurds.

At this point it should once again be emphasized that it is not sufficient to only look at the problem from a class perspective; it must also be examined from the ethnic perspective. Prof. Velidedeoğlu, for example, is regarded by the Turks as a respectable individual, important as a patriot, and a democrat. Nevertheless, due to his refusal to accept the existence of Kurds and their national struggle, in the eyes of the Kurdish population he is no more than an informer. He is a Turkish racist, one of the better spokesmen in defense of the official ideology of falsehoods, and enemy of Kurds and their struggle for national and democratic rights.

One of the major events in Northern Kurdistan which contributed substantially towards the development of national consciousness was the series of trials which took place under the regime of 12 March 1971. Known as the Eastern Trials, these were the trials where Kurds consciously and systematically defended their identities before the Turkish state. Their attitudes had a great deal of influence on Kurdish society. From the mid-

1970s onward, organizations with roots in the Revolutionary Cultural Associations of the East (*Devrimci Doğu Kültür Ocakları*) arose around various periodicals. These organizations included *Rizgari* (Revolution), *Özgürlük Yolu* (The Road to Freedom of the Revolutionary People's Cultural Association or *Devrimci Halk Kültür Derneği*), *Devrimci Demokrat* (Revolutionary Democrat of the Revolutionary Democratic Cultural Association), *Tekosin*, and *Kawa*, all of which published important publications. *Roja Welat* (Sun of the Homeland), *Roja Nu* were also important journals. Publishing houses such as Komal, Özgürlük Yolu, Koral, and Yöntem (Method), published studies on Kurdish history, language, literature, and social structure.

The Democratic Party of Kurdistan and the national liberators of Kurdistan played important roles in the reinterpretation and rewriting of Kurdish history. In the mid-1970s the thesis on colonialism was developed and defended by all Kurdish groups. The Turkish left, on the other hand, with the exception of a few groups such as Kurtuluş, came out against this thesis as a bloc. Political currents which were in stark opposition to each other made use of the same terminology and concepts to try and refute this view. This process also contributed towards the development of Kurdish national consciousness.

The founding of the PKK (*Partiya Karkari Kurdistan* or the Kurdistan Workers' Party) in the late 1970s, and the Second Eastern Trials which began under the regime of 12 September 1980, along with certain developments in Diyarbekir Prison, further contributed to the spread of Kurdish national consciousness. The PKK's armed struggle which began with the operations at Eruh and Shemdinli constituted a major turning point in the awakening of national consciousness and the comprehension of the thesis on colonialism. In the words of Franz Fanon, this was the "first bullet."

At this point it is worthwhile to take note of the resolution on the Kurdish Question passed by the Turkish Workers Party (*Türkiye İşçi Partisi* or TIP) in early 1970. At its Second Extraordinary Congress, the Turkish Workers Party passed a resolution that stated "The Kurds reside in the East of Turkey;" consequently, TIP was taken before the Constitutional Court and shut down. The leaders of the Turkish Workers Party were not very courageous in their defense of the resolution they had passed; they made a number of concessions to the official ideology and this brought about the need for a separate organization. However, the role of the Turkish Workers Party in the organization of the Eastern Demonstrations in various cities of the East in 1967 should not be forgotten either.

A large number of Kurdish intellectuals, revolutionaries, and fighters for democracy left Turkey for Europe following the military coup of 12 September 1980. These persons played a significant role in bringing the Kurdish issue to the attention of European and international democratic institutions. The Turkish army's repeated interventions in Southern Kurdistan since 25 May 1983, have been unequivocal indications of the international dimensions of the issue.

The numerous operations, massacres, and exiles, in short, colonialist practices, carried out by Turkey in Northern Kurdistan between 1925-1938 had been entirely ignored by the West. When such practices were carried out by the Turkish army in Southern Kurdistan on 25 May 1983, the situation was no longer as it was between 1925-1938. There was a reaction. Kurdistan is changing, and the increased sensitivity of Western public opinion is related to this change. Although the interest shown by the west is still far less than that shown in the Palestinian and Armenian questions, it still plays an important role in revealing the colonialist practices of Turkey in Kurdistan to the world at large.

Developments in Northern Kurdistan are significantly influenced by the national liberation struggles being waged in Southern and Eastern Kurdistan against Iraq and Iran respectively, and by the policies of these states, as well as Syria, towards Kurdish organizations. In the 1960s the Kurds were nowhere near being interested in the national liberation struggles being waged in Vietnam, Central America, or Palestine. But the peasant masses and craftsmen exhibited a closer interest in the Kurdish national liberation struggle.

The situation today is different. Kurds show great interest in events taking place in any region of Kurdistan. Everybody tries to find out as much as they can about events to comprehend the struggle. The movement's political and military successes generate great excitement, while its weakness and defeats brings forth widespread sorrow. All of this was clearly illustrated by the warmth and interest of Northern Kurds towards Southern Kurds who were forced to seek refuge in Northern Kurdistan when escaping assaults on them by chemical weapons.

The development of capitalism in Kurdistan, the breakup of tribal structures, and the decreasing influence of the institution of the sheikh, are all influential factors in bringing traditional social relations to an end. The people's national and democratic demands are coming to the forefront and becoming stronger with increases in numbers and productivity, the schooling of peasants, and the development of road networks and communications. Kurds follow other struggles for freedom and democracy in every corner of the world with close interest. The younger generation is beginning to question their predecessors on the subject of national identity.

The Turkish state is in close alliance with the traditional forces to prevent, slow down, or at least delay this rapid process of change. It is doing what it can to keep the tribal chiefs, sheikhs, and large landlords afloat, just as it has been doing since the founding of the Turkish Republic, although now in a more conscious fashion. Today, these reactionary institutions owe their existence to the Kemalists. The social weight of these traditional institutions have always been effective in slowing down the process of national awakening; when the Turkish secret services win over a sheikh or tribal chief, it's equal to establishing authority over thousands of people. The state also tries to keep the Kurdish movement under its control by drawing non-Kurds, particularly those of Arab origin, into its service.

Following the Dersim uprising of 1937-38, that is, once all the focal points of rebellion in Kurdistan had been done away with, the state presented the "Kurdish ruling classes" with two alternatives: they were either to take the side of the state, or they would be sent to the gallows like Sheikh Said and Seyid Rıza. Under these circumstances, the sheikhs, landlords, and tribal chiefs, in other words, the "Kurdish ruling classes," turned into agents for the Turkish government. At present, the majority of persons in this position cooperate with the government, which is still working to prevent this national awakening by establishing even closer alliances with the former, and lending them both financial and moral support. Among other benefits, the state grants them various types of credit, as well as licenses to distribute consumer goods, open petrol stations and so forth, so that these agents may increase their influence in their respective areas.

The major political parties, rather than building up local support through democratic methods, attempt to bring local populations under their influence by appointing influential Kurds as party heads. Such practices are a severe restriction on people's democratic demands. The conflict which broke out in the Social Democratic Populist Party (SHP) and led to an extraordinary congress in June 1989 was related to this subject. This meeting resulted in breaking off relations with influential party members, especially MPs who had close relations with their constituents and were acting as vehicles for reflecting the latter's revolutionary and democratic demands. Such MPs were replaced with new persons who stood for the official state ideology.

The Turk-Islam synthesis must also be understood within this context. In short, the aim of this movement is to dissolve the Kurdish national movement into Islamic internationalism. The sheikhs and religious officials are told that what is important is being Muslim, being human, being brothers. Ethnic feelings are contrary to Islam. This is now the official ideology transmitted through the sheikhs.

Religion is used to prevent the awakening of national feelings and anti-secularist activity is encouraged. The number and type of security forces are increased. New prisons are built. The number of police stations grows. So do their functions. The secret services are concentrated throughout the region. In spite of these developments, the region is still undergoing rapid change. Kurdistan is no longer what it used to be.

The Kurdish Issue and GAP

The state regards the Southeastern Anatolia Project (Güneydoğu Anadolu Projesi—GAP) as a significant investment in its plans to assimilate Kurds. The aim is to encourage western (Turkish) industrialists to make investments in the East through different incentive drives, such as tax reductions, facilitating the import of machinery, equipment, etc., with the hope that economic development results in the absorption of this region as it is connected to the West. The development of trade and industry would play a major role in spreading the Turkish language, as the local people are forced to use it as the dominant language in the development of economic relations with the West. Since Kurdish lacks the structure required to deal with economic, commercial, and industrial relations, it should gradually die out. Since it is a "primitive" language in the first place, it should be forgotten easily enough. So goes the logic.

The Turkish government's expectations will never be realized. Economic development and democratization will only serve to further accelerate the development of the national movement by supplanting traditional institutions. The deepening and spread of the movement is closely bound to the development of capitalism in the 1960s. The view that Kurdish is a primitive language that is insufficient to deal with growing economic and commercial relations is both mistaken and racist in its origins. Experts have indicated the wealth and potential of Kurdish.

Prohibitions against speaking and writing Kurdish, or references to it as primitive and lacking in literary value, is a malicious, hypocritical, and racist standpoint.

Furthermore, assimilation of Kurdish was brought to a halt as far back as the late 1960s with the founding of the Revolutionary Cultural Associations of the East. This is because Kurds living under oppression and tyranny became aware of their own true identities, began to wonder why they were not educated in their mother tongue, and questioned their government's role in their condition. People who undergo such a process and arrive at this level of consciousness can no longer be simply assimilated.

Numerous factors give rise to this sort of questioning. These include the rise in literacy, the influence of the mass media, the development of road networks, and the increase in means of communication and transportation at all levels. All of these facts have led to a more frequent interchange between individuals than was ever possible before. Although the basic function of institutions such as the schools, TV, radio, cinema, etc. is to accelerate and facilitate assimilation, they can also publicize the struggles for freedom, equality, and democracy throughout the world. The struggles occurring in South America, various parts of Asia, Palestine and elsewhere appear on TV and in the press. Reference is made to the presence of Turks in Bulgaria, Western Thrace, and Cyprus. Without ever mentioning the Kurds, they are in fact saying quite a lot, enabling the latter to gain a better understanding of the double standard being used against them, and the injustice to which they are subjected.

Colonialist methods can be said to have succeeded when they cause people to forget their mother tongue and prevent them from becoming conscious of this very process itself. Once the masses gain an awareness of what is going on and question this process, this means assimilation has come to a halt. Many of these people who were instrumental in the founding of the Revolutionary Cultural Associations of the East in the 1960s did not speak their mother tongue. According to the state, they had been assimilated. Nevertheless, having reached an awareness of their true identities, they felt the need to begin a struggle for democracy. Many of them later learned Kurdish, both spoken and written. Indeed, many of the individuals who got involved in publishing Kurdish journals did not speak Kurdish, but they had reached a consciousness and become activists.

Today a major portion of Kurds insist upon speaking Kurdish, their mother tongue, in courts, even though they know Turkish. In short, I am trying to point out the contrast in the Turkish government's expectations with regard to the assimilation of Kurds, and the wider processes that are taking place.

The "First Bullet" Theory

Franz Fanon participated in the Algerian National Liberation Struggle. He was a black man, born and raised in the French colony of Martinique, and studied medicine in Paris. In the early 1950s he became interested in the Algerian National Liberation Movement, and a few years later he succeeded in getting sent to that country as a doctor. Once there he was able to establish secret relations with the Algerian National Liberation Front.

Franz Fanon developed a thesis on colonial nations which is worthy of further examination. Briefly, his views are as follows: Organizing resistance in colonial nations and bringing them to the level of an armed struggle is very difficult, given that colonized people are conditioned to live in fear and intimidation. The colonial powers make them afraid and keep them under their control. Repression, force, tyranny, insults, and contempt bring on demoralization, causing the people to lose confidence in themselves and those around them, and to see their own relatives and nation as extraordinarily low and worthless. The colonial powers, on the other hand, appear so powerful that no one would even think of struggling against them. Colonized people become resigned to the fate forced upon them, putting themselves in the hands of God, rather than taking any action of their own.

The colonial state desires two things of those under its domination. First, for the colonized to recognize their rulers and think that they could not exist without their masters. The colonized should think that they are nothing but an unskilled, impoverished, lawless, ignorant people lacking all understanding of economics, administration, and technology. Second, while colonized people should stand silently with heads bowed before the harshest insults and contempt shown by the colonial powers, they should also be quick to react against the slightest insult or threat coming from their own relatives or countrymen, and turn such matters into issues of honor. This kind of social and moral environment creates aggressive and mean individuals, who waste their anger on their own relatives and countrymen.

The colonial powers exploit this psychological condition to the maximum. They deepen traditional conflicts within society, create new ones, while encouraging traditional institutions for their own ends. In the countryside, the security forces rape local women in front of their men, who are expected to stand silent. Nevertheless, when it comes down to conflicts between villages or tribes, these same people are encouraged to take revenge and "safeguard their honor."

The colonialist state employs people in possession of such mentalities in police stations, prisons, and torture chambers. All of this indicates how a colonized society is a wounded one. People and societies who do not rebel against tyranny and repression are wounded in their hearts.

Franz Fanon points out how difficult it is for people to organize and reach the point of war against the colonial power. He dwells on the necessity for overcoming this difficulty, and how concentrated, insistent, and decisive work is required to achieve results. He continues to say that all these negative conditions can be overcome, and anyone can be won to the organization. When this militant shoots his first bullet against the colonialist or imperialist state, he is actually killing himself. With that first bullet he kills his enslaved, terrorized, oppressed personality, giving birth to a new person. This new individual is one who has confidence in himself, his family, his fellow countrymen, and his nation. He no longer sees them as low and worthless. He no longer sees the colonial powers as overwhelming and omnipotent. He can now put everything in place, calculate his own strength and that of his enemy, and act accordingly.

"The first bullet" need not always come from a gun, but should be looked at from a wider angle. Its content can change according to time and place. An anti-colonialist publication could also serve the same function, given the right time and place.

State Terror in Kurdistan and Basis of Guerilla Warfare

A new generation is growing up in Kurdistan today. This new generation has seen their fathers and grandfathers beaten up, kicked around, insulted, and generally treated with contempt by the army, police, and gendarmerie. They have also witnessed their uncles and brothers thrown into dungeons and killed through torture. They have experienced their grandmothers, mothers, sisters and aunts dragged around by their hair, beaten up, and raped. This entire generation has witnessed their entire family being called "traitors," "bandits," "brigands," and "spineless." They have lived through such things on a daily basis. There is no way that this generation will not start questioning all of this within a very short time. All that has happened can not be forgotten. The only thing which has meaning at this point is the struggle for identity and a human life.

Those who founded the Revolutionary Cultural Associations of the East in 1968, those who were tried in the 1971 Eastern Trials, were the same bare-bottomed, snotty children with bloated bellies of the 1950s so often portrayed in the Turkish press. The children who were raised in the 1960s on the myths of the "Great Turks," only to see their grandfathers and fathers paraded around the villages naked with strings tied to their genitals.

These children, the guerrillas of today, are certainly no longer regarded with the same affection by Turkish intellectuals and the press as they were when they were naked and snotty-nosed!

In the 1971 Eastern Trials, those being tried said, "Today you can hardly fit us all into your courtroom. In the future we'll be so many that you won't even be able to fit us into your stadiums." Today all prisons are filled beyond capacity. The struggle, however, continues and has been carried over into the countryside; it echoes through the mountains and valleys.

The Material and Psychological Basis of Guerilla Warfare

But the guerrilla movement must not be taken as a reactionary movement, a kind of revenge for the situation described above. It is my opinion that it would be more correct to view this movement as a road towards the eradication of colonialism. Guerrilla activity is taken up once it is realized that this type of denigration and mistreatment stems from colonialism, from which liberation is the only solution. The guerrilla struggle is a product of the rise in political consciousness. Its aim is to remove all traces of colonial oppression.

Mao said that an idea with which the popular masses identified and were organically connected represented a great strength. The greatest material force is for an idea to be taken on by the popular masses. Such a force can not be destroyed by guns or cannonballs. This is why it is vital for a nation to question its present and past. Such a process brings about a rise in political and social consciousness. Once a nation has begun to question, to ask itself, "Who are we?," then that nation has already covered a great distance towards national liberation.

The Negative Influence of the Official State Ideology

Kurds have inevitably suffered from the effects of daily propaganda assaults, such as the greatness of Turks, the mere fact of being a Turk bringing one great happiness, assertions that Kurds will never be more than slaves, dependent on others, traitors, bandits, and cowards, etc. This is even more true given that this official ideology is enforced by repression, beatings, and torture. Nevertheless, the negative effects of the official state ideology also assists in breaking the chains of slavery.

By now those states which have mutually colonized Kurdistan, as well as various other international institutions which aim to protect human rights, such as the United Nations, the Council of Europe, the European Parliament, and the Helsinki Final Accords (Conference for Security and Cooperation in Europe) should be aware that Kurdistan is not what it used to be. By pretending not to see what is going on, the United Nations is actually defending Kurdistan's less than colonial status. This makes the United Nations a non-functional and rotten organization.

The Islamic Conference can be looked at within the same context. Despite all its denunciations of Israel, and proposals for international sanctions on account of Israel's oppression of the Palestinians, it pretends to be unaware of the even harsher policies to which the Kurds are subjected. By maintaining a double standard, it will never obtain results. Israel, for one, will never take the Islamic Conference seriously as long as the Palestinians possess more rights than the Kurds. What answer can the Islamic states give for the atrocities committed against the Kurds? Such double standards prevent these organizations from functioning effectively.

Furthermore, it should not be forgotten that Kurdish society is itself a Muslim society. Organizations such as the Islamic Conference have to try exceptionally hard to overlook this issue. Nevertheless, it is becoming harder for them to remain deaf and mute. Such contradictory practices and attitudes are now addressed more often and brought up for discussion.

The destruction of both nature and humanity in Kurdistan is aimed at breaking down the people's psychological structure and destroying their will. Kurds are meant to be overcome by constant fear and panic, a sense of powerlessness, and a lack all confidence in the future of their nation. These practices aim at eradicating their customs and language, breaking all their resistance, so that they are incapable of doing anything but submitting to the will of their masters. This is how the colonialists want their subjects to live. This is the basis of colonialist-colonial relations. Economic exploitation can only be carried out within such an environment of moral and psychological despair.

Turkey has attempted to further deepen its policy of "divide, rule, and liquidate" through setting up a system of "village guards" in the face of the unchecked upsurge in the activity of the Kurdish guerrillas. Along with the village guards, the violence that is endemic to the colonial society is directed towards the guerrillas, their relatives, and their villages. In the face of every possible type of state terror, tyranny, torture, and oppression, any who still stand up and defend Kurdish identity are then physically annihilated. The violence and aggression of the colonial army is increasing from day to day. The state practices every sort of terrorism it can conceive of. Villages are besieged, entire villages are searched, mass torture is practiced, human beings are hunted down like animals, concentration camps are formed, poisonous gas is released into urban areas and water sources, people are exiled, and far more. Provocateurs and spies arc planted amongst the villagers.

Colonialist states can confiscate Kurdish property, including land and livestock, at any time. They can send in armed soldiers to settle in villages. They can force villagers to sow and reap for their own use. They can hold the villagers accountable for regional security and demand that they stand guard in turns. They can demand that families turn over any of their own who may have joined the guerrillas, and if the former refuse to do so, every one of them is subject to arrest and questioning. They take great pains to make the villagers themselves pay for expenses incurred for the latter's security. Those who speak up against such measures can be shot. Those who accept such methods, on the other hand, lower their own self worth. They become characterized by shame and fear. In either of the above cases, the state has achieved its objective.

Training in all of the above activities is done by experts, especially foreign ones. They are counter insurgency activities.

The Failure of the Official Ideology

The only policy Turkey has regarding the Kurdish issue is state terrorism. Their aim is to terrorize to such a degree that no-one even dares to bring up the issue of Kurdish national and democratic rights. This means enforcing such severe repression that people know that not only they themselves, but their entire families, tribes, and villages will be penalized for any action they may undertake. Nevertheless, despite all of this torture, killing and deprivation, research and study on Kurdistan, the Kurdish language, and Kurdish culture are increasing from day to day. Demand for national and democratic rights is on the rise. Assimilation has been halted ever since the founding of the Revolutionary Cultural Associations of the East. Economic development and democratization will only serve to further accelerate the development of Kurdish national consciousness. The fact that the struggle is spreading and becoming more intense, despite all the state's policies of terrorization, signifies that such policies have, in fact, become bankrupt. They no longer function. And the government has no alternative policy.

I would also like to bring up the attitudes of both İlhan Selçuk and Nadire Mater on another issue. Nadire Mater asked İlhan Selçuk what his views were on the PKK. The latter said that his opinion on the subject was negative and outlined the reasons why. There was a lack of scientific objectivity in the question and answer. Given the official ideology and legal situation in Turkey today, it is not possible to come up with a sound and objective interpretation of the "PKK phenomenon." All the interpretations on the subject are nothing more than repetition of the official state views, which are a slander. The state accuses the PKK of being a "network of crime," "a bloodthirsty gang," an organization which "indiscriminately murders men, women, children, young and old," "bandits," "a gang of brigands," etc. In a country where to speak in favor of the PKK is a crime carrying a stiff punishment, it is not very scientific to spew out a mouthful of curses against them. All one is doing is repeating the official view of the state. Nor is this a moral attitude. Given the circumstances, it is the duty of progressive Turks and the press to fight for conditions where expressing positive views on the PKK, as well as negative views on Ataturk and Ataturkism, are not considered an offence.

General Necip Torumtay's statement of 17 August 1989, that all who support and take the side of the PKK are to be declared "enemies" should be regarded at within the same framework. Given these circumstances, it is not possible to have a healthy approach to the events taking place in the East without being prepared to take certain risks.

What comes to mind here is Voltaire's statement, "I disagree with what you say, but I will defend to the death your right to say it."

Nadire Mater was wrong in posing such a question since it was already obvious what the answer would be. İlhan Selçuk was wrong in not responding that it is wrong to ask questions about organizations when speaking in their favor constitutes a crime.

To demonstrate how big a crime it is to speak in favor of the PKK, one should take a look at the case which was opened against Mehdi Zana, former Mayor of Diyarbekir, who made a statement which was printed in the newspaper *Cumhuriyet* saying that he supported the national liberation movement of the PKK (*Cumhuriyet*, 3 August 1988). He was tried in a military court and sentenced to 5-10 years in prison.

In addition to the above, I would also like to point out that İlhan Selçuk has denounced the Members of Parliament coming from the East for not putting forth demands for national democratic rights. In fact, Turkish writers and intellectuals have praised those MPs of Kurdish origin for not putting forth national demands, and not resisting assimilation. These writers and intellectuals have stated that the Kurdish MPs in question have defended the Turkish state and the Turkish nation as much (or more) than Turks themselves. These Kurdish MPs are encouraged to continue their work, which is said to be progressive, revolutionary, and democratic.

No matter how much the denial of national identity is praised by the writers, journalists, and administrators of the ruling Turkish nation, they will always be remembered with hatred and disgust in the future. A similar fate awaits the MPs of Kurdish origin in the not too distant future. The social dynamic in Kurdistan is progressing much faster than is realized and is forcing everyone to take a position on one side or the other.

The Visible Result of Guerilla Warfare

Northern Kurdistan has undergone two radical changes since guerrilla activity began by the PKK on 14-15 August 1984, in Eruh and Shemdinli. The first of these is that the guerrilla movement was itself transformed. Fear and intimidation were replaced by determination, consciousness, and struggle. Such an attitude gained supporters for the movement and institutionalized both the struggle and the guerrilla movement. Today this movement is a significant part of the struggle, and a force recognized by the Kurdish popular masses for its role in fighting against the Turkish security forces and the army.

Following the coup of 12 September 1980, political prisoners began undergoing hunger strikes to protest against the repression and tyranny to which they were subjected, and to make the public aware of the horrible conditions in which they were forced to live. When confronted with these hunger strikes, the officers in charge of prison security would say with rage and hatred: "The army, the state, gives you food. How can you dare to refuse it?" The officers were not in the least interested in the prisoners' health: they were outraged because their orders were not being obeyed. In their eyes, those who carried out hunger strikes were guilty of lowering the army's prestige.

When the guerrillas began to reply to calls to surrender by opening fire and going into battle, and fighting these battles with determination for however many days or weeks they might last, this was a sure indication that they had changed. Along with them, the local population began to change as well. This was the second radical change in Kurdistan. People accustomed to living in fear and intimidation began to rebel, to stand up and demand their rights. Although guerrilla activity may not achieve its desired results in the short term, the fact that people's psychological make up has been transformed is of extreme significance. The people in some regions of Kurdistan have already begun to demand equality and democracy, as well as to compare their great deprivation to others. Such changes are the results of this resolute and conscious struggle, which is being accompanied by political and ideological action. The repercussions this activity has created on both the national and international level should not be underestimated.

Twenty or thirty years ago if any Kurdish peasant in the regions of Bitlis, Diyarbekir or elsewhere were to be questioned on what he thought of Kurdish national rights, he would generally give an answer resembling the following: "Sir, we're all Muslims, brothers in faith; whether or not we speak Kurdish doesn't really matter. The state doesn't want to give Kurds any rights, and it's not going to. The Kurds are weak, and the state is powerful. Fighting for things like this would just wear us out, destroy us. If the state provides us with roads, schools, and water, that is enough." When it was brought out that since Kurdish rights could not be achieved through peaceful means, struggle is necessary, and that the right to speak and write in one's native tongue is a fundamental right worth fighting for, reactions were stronger. The reply would be along the following lines, "Sir, to fight the state, a state is necessary. We are a poor and ignorant people. The Turkish state is great and powerful, with a big army, airplanes, tanks, cannons and guns. The government has its police, prisons, schools, newspapers, radios, and everything else. What have we got? Nothing. How can we wage a struggle in such conditions? The best thing we can do is to stay put." If one was insistent on the subject of the Kurds' national and democratic rights, the reply would be, "We are right, we are completely in the right, but we have no strength, no-one to stand up for us, no friends." This is the crushed psychological condition which the guerrilla movement did away with.

By replying to the call to surrender with gunshots, those guerrillas who both killed and were killed played a major role in their nation's confidence in itself. People see the great self-sacrifice of the guerrillas, recognizing them as a significant force against the government's security forces. Confidence and trust in them increases from day to day.

Another indication of the transformation of attitudes is the way the people claim the bodies of those killed by the army and other security forces, organize their funerals, and pay visits to their relatives to express their condolences. In the early years of the guerrilla activity, people were too afraid to retrieve their dead from the hands of the state. They were afraid of the questioning and torture to which they would be subjected if they made it known that they were related to the dead guerrilla. Bodies were left on the mountains to be collected by the security forces and dumped into pits.

In the beginning, in fact, the army did not even want the people to claim their dead, so as to create the image that the guerrillas were nothing but a handful of looters with no connections to the people, rejected even by their own families. They used this image to spread propaganda that there was no popular support for the guerrilla movement. This situation has changed in the last few years. Now the people claim their dead from the army. To the charge that the dead guerrillas were traitors and brigands, they now answer that the guerillas in question were patriots. When they succeed in claiming the bodies they hold funeral ceremonies in the villages and bury them.

When one of the "village guards" (villagers employed by the state to inform on guerrilla activity in the region) is killed, there are not even enough villagers who can be rounded up to carry the coffin. No-one comes to pay condolences to the family. The funerals of guerrillas, to the contrary, draw great crowds, and those killed are referred to as martyrs.

In Yılmaz Güney's film *Yol*, there is a striking scene of a battle between gendarmes and smugglers, in which the bodies of the dead smugglers are thrown into a trailer and taken to the village. The commander of the gendarmerie unit gathers all the villagers around the trailer and instructs them to pick out their dead relations. No-one admits to knowing anyone in the trailer; they say the faces of the dead are foreign to them. In fact, the dead men are all well-known locals, but the villagers are afraid to claim them because they fear the interrogation and torture to which they will be subjected as relatives of the dead smugglers. This is the kind of alienation brought on through colonialism which causes people to deny their own identities.

Obviously the state is very disturbed by the support the guerrillas receive from the people. This is why the government has made a major change in tactics lately. Rather than expend all of their energy on the PKK members themselves, they direct their efforts towards catching those who support and give shelter and provisions to the PKK. In this way they try to isolate the guerrillas from the masses. By trying to place agents provocateurs amongst the guerrillas and creating informers, they are able to arrest and interrogate hundreds, even thousands of people. They use such methods to try to lower the esteem held for the guerrillas by the local peasants and traders. Moreover, they try to terrorize the villagers through cruel torture, even taking recourse to such insults to human dignity as forcing people to eat human excrement. The aim of such practices is to destroy human dignity, create an atmosphere of panic, and crush the will to resist.

The "village guards," with the extraordinary powers they possess, are employed to spy on and terrorize villagers and tradesmen who are PKK members or supporters. In addition to their salaries they are paid high rewards for any PKK members they kill, with the amount varying according to the rank of the victim. They are even authorized to burn the homes of guerrillas and their supporters, destroy their belongings, slaughter their livestock, burn their crops, and kidnap their women. Amongst these guards are many common criminals who were either in prison, or have escaped from prison. The state has either released them or pardoned their escape, as well as given them weapons, in exchange for their work as paid informers. Nevertheless, despite such tyranny, the guerrilla movement continues to spread.

The Kurds' opportunities to compare their situation with that of other societies around them are continually increasing. In the *Belene* series broadcast on television in June 1989, they were able to put themselves in the place of the Turks living in Bulgaria. The atrocities experienced in Diyarbekir prison in the early eighties came alive before their eyes in the portrayal of the tyranny to which the Turks in Bulgaria are subjected. The confiscation of the identity papers of a village teacher, and the trouble which ensued was another example. In Kurdistan villagers are often subject to such mistreatment. The series also showed how a prisoner in solitary confinement lost his mind and died on account of the rats circulating in the sewers. In Diyarbekir, the prisoners were forced to eat rats. A number of them then had all of their teeth pulled out as a consequence after they were released.

The officers and secret service agents in the *Belene* series frequently shouted the word, "unity, unity, unity!" which is known to be one of the favorite slogans of the 12th September regime, and goes back to the days of the founding of the Republic. The series also shows how circumcision ceremonies of Turks are carried out in secret in Bulgaria. Great efforts were spent on trying to circumcise Armenians in prisons following the coup of 12th September.

The series portrayed how Turkish villages in Bulgaria were frequently raided. Village raids, sieges, and searches are every day events in Kurdistan. The *Belene* series showed how the properties of Turks in Bulgaria were frequently confiscated by the Bulgarian government. In Kurdistan, soldiers, special teams, and village guards confiscate the property of Kurdish villagers any time they want. The series frequently referred to the fact that Turks were forced to change their names and take on Bulgarian ones. In Turkey, the prohibition of Kurdish names is a fundamental policy of the state. Another event depicted in this series was how Turks were forced to worship in secret, how they were victims of religious repression. What about the repressive measures taken by the 12th September regime to force Alevis to go to mosques?

Furthermore, the *Belene* series pointed out how Turks in Bulgaria could only gain access to equal treatment through assuming Bulgarian identities. In Turkey, equal treatment is contingent upon being a Turk. Although the Turkish press, government officials, spokesmen for the Trade Union Türk İş, and all sorts of other official associations are quick to rush to the defense of the Turkish minority in Bulgaria, when it comes to Kurds, they somehow manage to see and hear nothing.

There is no doubt that the changes in mentality and attitude now spreading throughout Kurdistan are also influencing the attitudes and ideas of their representatives in Ankara. Members of Parliament of Kurdish origin are trying to bring up the issue of people's national and democratic desires. The major political parties such as the Social Democratic Party (SHP), True Path Party (DYP), and Motherland Party (ANAP), on the other hand, who define their views and actions along the lines of institutions such as the army and the national intelligence organization (MIT)—rather than in accordance with the desires of the Kurdish people—are doing their best to drown the desires coming from their constituents. They are certainly well versed in the methods for doing so.

Colonialist Practices and Turkish Intellectuals

The attitude and actions of French intellectuals during the Algerian War of National Liberation, one of the bloodiest wars of national liberation in history, with over a million dead, was a very honorable one. Many of them took the side of the Algerian National Liberation Front and openly criticized the colonialist practices of their own government. The preface to Franz Fanon's book, *The Wretched of the Earth*, for example, written by Jean Paul Sartre, turned the minds of the French upside down.

One should not mistake such attitudes as belonging to all French people, although they definitely represented a strong current. Although not large in numbers, their voices conveyed an influential force. Associations for the assistance of the Algerian National Liberation Front were set up at French universities, despite the risks and repression it entailed. Many of those working in these associations were university professors. There were incidents where professors resigned in protest against the colonialist practices and atrocities of the French government. Articles in favor of the Algerian National Liberation Front often appeared in the French press, pointing out how wrong it was for the French to be in Algeria. Demonstrations, protest marches, conferences, panel discussions, and forums came out against the French imperialist and colonialist policies and practices of the French government in Algeria. Numerous doctors, engineers, teachers and technicians participated in the Front. French churches also gave assistance to liberation fighters.

Such an attitude is not particular to the French. Many Americans came out against their own government's policies in Vietnam and defended the right of the Vietcong. There was also a section of the Jewish population of Israel which criticized the Israeli government for its assault on Lebanon and the PLO in the summer of 1982. Large demonstrations were held in Tel-Aviv and Jerusalem. The existence of such Jews today who defend the PLO and criticize their own government is a great credit to humanity. The fact that they are not branded as traitors, thrown into prison, and tortured is a point in Israel's favor.

Turkish universities are far removed from such attitudes. They remain one of the major institutions for the propagation of the official Turkish ideology, which is based on falsehood. The Turkish universities' methods of operation resemble parts of the Turkish national intelligence agency (MIT) more than they do institutions of knowledge. Should anyone in the universities undertake research on the subject of Kurdistan, he is immediately relieved of duty. All the Turkish universities do is spread propaganda that Kurds are in reality Turks, and that there is no such language as Kurdish in existence.

The same can be said for the Turkish press and political parties. Again, they operate like subdivisions of the national intelligence organisation. For example, when an entire village is rounded up and tortured in a village school, it's not mentioned in the press. If, however, there happens to be an attack on the school, if this torture center is burned, they raise a big fuss by writing articles with titles such as "PKK burns another school."

Human rights' associations have been established in various official institutions, such as at certain universities, throughout Turkey. Unfortunately, their behavior is not much different from other Turkish organizations described above. As for human rights' associations which have been set up by intellectuals outside of official institutions, they have not yet issued statements on the Kurdish issue. They pretend to be unaware of it. Turkish intellectuals, far from taking the side of Kurdish fighters for national liberation, applaud the government's racist and colonialist policies with all their might.

The human rights associations in Turkey consider it a great virtue to be bound to the values held sacred by the Turkish state, as if they were living in a country without a Kurdish issue to deal with. They do not even show a fraction of the interest they give to the PLO, or the Turkish minority in Bulgaria. As a result of their double standard, not much of what they do achieves any concrete result.

"Turkish intellectuals," with all their passion for freedom and culture, must know by now that they hold a dominant position over another nation which has less than a colonial status. For the sake of more freedom for Turks, for Turkish ideals, and for Turkish culture, every day crimes are committed and Kurds are murdered in that colony.

The Need for Scientific Research

Science and research based on facts are the most important methods the human mind has for comprehending the world. The official ideology of the Turkish state, however, goes completely contrary to fact. The heavy sanctions imposed on persons who bring up issues not accepted by the state ideology show that the environment in Turkey is not conducive to the furtherance of scientific inquiry. Only when a person can defend his views, or when all views can be criticized openly, can we say that there is an environment conducive to the furthering of science.

Living in accordance with the official ideology goes against the concept of civilization. Civilization includes the freedom to criticize government policies without being penalized. This is the underlying concept of Western Civilization. Human rights and civil liberties can only flourish under such conditions. Science can only flourish in such an environment. This means a political system and society where there is no institutionalized official ideology.

Part II

Reflections on the "Kurdish Ruling Class"

Introduction

Scientific studies are commissioned by those who have need of them. Kurds have a great need for such studies because the states which control them have done all they can to prevent the subject of Kurds being investigated in an objective fashion. All documentation under the control of hostile states has either been destroyed or made inaccessible. The documents presented to the public have clearly been doctored. On the other hand, much of the work which has so far been undertaken has not gone beyond the framework of official state ideologies. This holds true for most of the research done by Turks. Clearly, if sound research is to be undertaken, it must be done by the Kurds themselves.

The past and present of Kurdish society must be studied thoroughly. Kurdish society's inner dynamics and the external factors bearing upon them must be investigated with as much factual evidence as possible. In this study we will try to advance some ideas related to the subject of Kurdish ruling classes.

A Worn Out Phrase

It is generally accepted, especially in left wing circles, that Turkey is ruled by a Turkish and Kurdish ruling class. In the programs of the Turkish Workers Party and National Democratic Revolution in the 1960s, as well as in those of the socialist parties and political movements of the 1970s, Eastern categories such as landlords, sheikhs, and tribal chieftains were considered as ruling classes. In my opinion, this point of view is mistaken. I think that although landlords, sheikhs and tribal chieftains can be categorized as part of the ruling class block, they should not be referred to as the ruling class. They are better considered as agents. The same can be said for the merchant and industrial sectors. None of the persons included in the above categories holds any authority when it comes to determining the economic and social policies applied in Kurdistan. The only thing they do is to apply what has been decided on by the Turkish government in accordance with the latter's own interests, and perform whatever duties are required in relation to these decisions. They are rewarded, both materially and otherwise, in proportion to how thoroughly they execute these duties.

This is why the thought and action of this category of people can not be expressed by the concept of a ruling class.

This study deals with how the "Kurdish ruling class" turned into a class of agents and the consequences of this process, which is one of the most important aspects of Kurdistan's economic and social history. The states which rule Kurdistan have always done away with rebellious elements, and expended great amounts of energy on forming a class willing to collaborate with themselves. We can say that those who resisted or considered resisting were the strongest and most dynamic sectors of Kurdish society. This is why this process has led to a decrease in the social strength of Kurds. The collaborating sector, on the other hand, has increased in influence with time, and constitutes a new focal point of resistance. The various governments which rule Kurdistan, however, do not intend to allow this potential center of resistance the possibility of further increasing its power, and are in the process of breaking it up and liquidating it. This means a further reduction in the strength of Kurdish society, as well as paving the way for increased collaboration.

At this point we ought to clarify a point on the concept of class. Class is a concept related to production and the ownership of the means of production. In the present era, there are two main classes, the bourgeoisie and the working class. Categories such as bureaucrats, intellectuals, peasants, etc. are not classes. They can be referred to as groups, sectors, layers, and so on. By this definition, the collaborators in Kurdistan are also not a class. They are lacking in the continuity and permanency inherent in the concept of class. Most of the time, the younger generations are unwilling to carry on in the same function of their fathers and grandfathers as agents. They even feel ashamed of what their fathers have done. Nevertheless, I refer to this category as an "agent" class in the same vein as is common in the vernacular Turkish coining of such phrases as "technocrat class." I could not have said "agent sector," because people from all different sectors such as landlords, sheikhs, merchants, building contractors, high ranking bureaucrats, civil servants, students, writers, journalists and so on are included. "Agent class" includes all of those who perform this role.

On the other hand, pre-capitalist relations of production are predominant in Kurdistan. Even though, due to capitalism's rapid development, one cannot speak of a feudal class, it is possible to speak of "feudal remains." We should point out that acting as agents is not a result of the disintegration of feudal relations and the development of capitalist relations. I have tried to make it clear that it is the pre-capitalist classes which have become agents. This process advanced with the establishment and development of capitalist relations. Capitalist development can only take place alongside such a process.

Another significant dimension of Kurdish history is the fact that the country lies at a significant historical crossroads. Repeated invasions and divisions have prevented the formation of a centralized and stable Kurdish authority. Another factor which has played a role in recent history is the presence of natural resources, petroleum in particular.

The Ottoman State became aware of these factors in relation to Kurdistan in the nineteenth century. This awareness gradually became clearer until it crystallized along with the formation of the Young Turk movement. Towards the end of the nineteenth century the Ottomans also became aware that they would no longer be able to hold onto the Balkans. The spread of ideas about the French Revolution throughout Europe accelerated the withdrawal of the Ottomans from the Balkans. When it came to Armenia, Kurdistan, and Arabia, however, the Ottomans were unable to show the same flexibility. Plans were developed for incorporating these countries as organic parts of the state, and efforts were undertaken towards the realization of these plans.

Following World War I, we witnessed the imperialist struggle for the division of Kurdistan between British imperialists and Kemalists. The aim of this struggle was to see who could get a bigger share of Kurdistan. This meant that in essence the struggle was between an objective alliance of British imperialists and Kemalists on the one hand, and the Kurds on the other. This was how things in fact really were. The alliance between British imperialists and Kemalists, however, was much stronger than is generally supposed. Political and ideological propaganda have obscured the real dimensions of the issue. Certain superficial matters appear as the determining factors. The Kurds' desires for freedom and independence were drowned in blood. The Kemalist fight to get a bigger share of Kurdistan is portrayed as an anti-imperialist struggle.

French and other imperialist powers, such as Iran and the Arab colonialists played a secondary role in the struggle for the division of Kurdistan. At a time when the principle of the right of nations to self-determination was embracing all of Asia, the Middle East and North Africa, Kurdistan was carved up and shared out. The Bolsheviks watched this process and sometimes backed the Kemalists.

This struggle over Kurdistan was one of the most important events that took place in the Middle East between 1915-1925. Nevertheless the Kemalists, to gain the support of Kurds in their wars against the

Armenians and Greeks between 1915-1925, were obliged to make certain concessions. They promised that following victory in the war against the "infidels" Kurds would receive national rights. In my opinion this was a mere tactic which was not carried out following victory over Armenians and Greeks. It was simply forgotten.

The reasons for the policy of divide and rule applied to Kurds, the manner in which this policy was carried out, and the results of this policy are outside the scope of this study. We are only attempting to look into the relationships which resulted from these policies in terms of the development of nationalist thought, ruling classes, and the class basis of the Kurdish national movement.

One of the major issues for the newly founded Turkish Republic was the full incorporation of Northern Kurdistan into the body of the Turkish state. In Young Turk thought and action, this was the highest achievement for the Committee for Union and Progress. This is why, from the mid 1920s on, the Kurds' national aspirations began to be drowned in blood. As was seen in Kochgiri, this began as early as late 1920. The Kurds who rebelled demanding national rights were debilitated through the gallows, internal and foreign exile, massacres, and outright genocide. This of course happened over time. The beginning was the Sheikh Said rebellion in 1925. A number of uprisings took place in various locations in 1927, 1930-32, 1934, and 1935. All were repressed through bloodshed. All resulted in massacre and exile. The last of these was the Dersim rebellion, which resulted in genocide. Genocide was also carried out in 1929, and between 1930-32 in the Zilan valley.

Throughout this period, Kurdish resistance continued against the British, Arab, and Persian colonialists in Southern and Eastern Kurdistan.

The Kurds Facing State Oppression

The 1937-38 Dersim uprising was repressed through genocidal measures, and resulted in suppression of all points of resistance throughout Northern Kurdistan. All potential centers of rebellion were broken up and Kurdistan began to be absorbed as an organic part of the Turkish Republic. This absorption led to the collection of taxes and recruitment of soldiers on a regular basis, as well as the penetration of the Turkish State in every nook and cranny of Kurdish society. This included the introduction of a Turkish system of education and the spread of Turkish culture through every available channel. These developments led to the detachment of the Kurdish masses from their roots, and their assimilation into Turkish society. The state gave the Kurdish ruling classes, such as sheikhs, tribal chieftains and large landowners two choices: Either renounce your Kurdish identities and become Turks or, like Sheikh Said, Sheikh Rıza, and others, prepare for the gallows. There was no other option.

The denial of one's Kurdish identity and the adoption of Turkish identity is not a simple or passive process. It also involves the active collaboration with the Turkish security forces as de facto agents of the government. It implies working against those who refuse to do so, those who defend Kurdish rights. Consequently, following the 1940s, the majority of the large landowners, tribal chiefs, and sheikhs turned into agents and began working against the Kurdish national movement.

It would be useful to separate the two kinds of sheikhs, landlords, and tribal chiefs. First were those who cared for and spoke out in defence of Kurdistan. They tried to do something and risked losing their lives on the gallows. In the second category were those who completely denied their Kurdish identity and even went so far as to make Turkish propaganda. Such collaborators have been around since the early 1920s. They were even active in the final years of the Ottoman Empire. The people in this second category have always been rewarded for what they have done. For instance, they were appointed to the Turkish parliament by the leader of the Republican People's Party and President of the Republic of Turkey, Mustafa Kemal. Following the 1940s, such collaboration was solicited more systematically and advanced by the use of state terror, internal exile, and confiscation of property.

To take one example, we can contrast Sheikh Said and Sheikh Ibrahim Arvasi. Sheikh Said was executed for his defence of Kurdistan and while hanging he expressed his hopes for the future of Kurdistan. After he had been hung, his family was exiled and his property confiscated. Sheikh Ibrahim Arvasi, on the other hand, denied his national identity and fully accepted the official Turkish ideology. He even helped to spread the latter. Arvasi was made a member of the Turkish parliament by Mustafa Kemal and later on by İsmet İnönü. Arvasi was also rewarded with material goods and prestige. Such persons were encouraged to take possession of the estates left by Armenians and exiled Kurds. Sheikh Ibrahim Arvasi was made a member of the Turkish parliament in 1920 and 1923, and then in 1927, 1931, and 1935 until 1950. Kurdish landlords, sheikhs and tribal chieftains, who cooperated with the Turkish state, increased their influence over local Kurdish populations by being appointed to the Turkish parliament during the period of single party rule. They spread the official Turkish ideology and propaganda, and accelerated the denial of Kurdish identity.

How have traditional institutions like landlords, sheikhs and tribal chieftains managed to survive until the present day? In my opinion, it is because the Kemalists, or in other words, the Turkish state, wants them to survive. Every measure is taken to prevent them from dying out, because once they do so, the Kurdish masses will rapidly become conscious of their Kurdish identities. They will begin to demand national rights. They will compare their situation with that of other nations. The reason the system of village guards is stronger in Hakkari than in other areas, for instance, is because the tribal system is stronger there. The chief of a tribe can easily distribute guns amongst all the members of his tribe and ensure they all act as "guards." It is sufficient that one chief turns into an agent for all the rest of the tribe to follow suit. On the other hand, once the tribal system is broken up, people will be able to think and act independently of the various landlords and tribal chiefs.

The ban on the Kurdish language is another factor which has contributed to the survival of these institutions. If a Kurd, forbidden to speak his own language, needs to communicate with government agencies or police, he will obviously require the assistance of someone who speaks Turkish. Let's not forget that until the 1950s the only people who knew Turkish in Kurdistan, even though they did not know it very well, were the sheikhs, chiefs, and landlords. This meant that they were the only means available for communicating with the land deeds bureau, the tax department, the Public Registration Office, local government officials, lawyers, courts, and so on. Along with their social and economic functions these traditional authorities also became bridges between the people and the state. Ordinary Kurds had no choice but to rely on them and hope they would take care of things...

The institutions of tribe and sheikh are of great significance for the Kurdish national liberation struggle. It is said that they must either be won over or destroyed. Given what we have outlined above, we can say that our attitude towards them may vary according to time and place. In general, however, we must try to eradicate this type of reactionary institutions. It is too easy for them to be manipulated by the government. The latter has access to all sorts of powers to bribe and coerce them. The advantages of the spread of democracy will help to put an end to these institutions, which are major obstacles to social and political progress.

The Transformation of the Class Struggle in Kurdistan in the Nineteenth Century

For research purposes, the economic and social order of Kurdistan can be broken down into various periods: the pre-Islamic period; the transformation following conversion to Islam; the period of the Oghuz Turks; the Seljuk period; post 1514; the Ottoman and Persian Empires, and so on.

There is one characteristic of the Kurdish social, economic and political structure throughout these periods which must be kept in mind: there are significant differences between classical European feudalism on the one hand, and oriental-Islamic and Kurdish-Islamic feudalism on the other. Under European feudalism, the power of the church was different from those of the feudal lords. The powers which sprung from the relations of production and those which originated in the church were not in the same hands. In contrast, under Kurdish-Islamic feudalism, religious power went hand in hand with that derived from the relations of production. In Kurdistan, the Mir (chief, leader) was at the head of the religious hierarchy. Production was often in the hands of the sheikh or tribal chief.

The latter handled religious affairs in God's name. They recited the noon prayers at the mosque. They had others recite in their names. They were God's representatives on earth. Since the duties of the church were separate from those of the feudal lords in the West, the church was not an institution with legal authority over the relations of production. As a result, as feudalism broke up in the West, the Church did not defend it as an everlasting order. In Kurdish-Islamic feudalism, as in all Oriental-Islamic feudalism, since the religious institutions were in the hands of the Mirs or lords, religion played a reactionary function impeding the progress of the relations of production to a higher level. Religion tried to legitimize feudal exploitation. Therefore, while the separation between religion and production resulted in the liquidation of feudalism in Europe, the lack of separation in Kurdish-Islamic feudalism ensured the continuity of feudalism.

In Kurdistan, tribes were independent units. Nevertheless, there were periods during which the tribes were bound to a particular Mir. The Mirs drew their power either from tribal chieftaincy, or from their religious functions. In addition to this were the titles of privilege and edicts granted by the Abbasid, Persian, and Ottoman monarchs. Under these titles and edicts, administration and income in a particular district were left to the

Mir. Although this did not mean full ownership of the land, it meant a large degree of influence and control. This authority could also be passed on from father to son. Mirs who lacked the right to control land drew their strength from taxes and tithes. Mirs were independent governments. Due to their widespread political and religious powers, it was not necessary for them to actually own the land. This was more or less the way things were until the nineteenth century when there began a major transformation in the traditional class structure.

From the early part of the nineteenth century there were intense struggles between Kurds and the Ottoman State. Having been forced to retreat from the Balkans, the Ottoman State turned all its forces towards maintaining a strong hold in Kurdistan, Armenia, the Arab lands and Anatolia. Attempts were made to incorporate Kurdistan as an organic part of the empire. This was done through the recruitment of soldiers and collection of taxes. The Ottoman State organized countless expeditions into the area to ensure the realization of these two goals, which were met with hostility on the part of the Kurds. Endless and bitter battles were fought, led by the Kurdish feudal lords, the Mirs. The Mirs were a class of landed aristocracy in Kurdistan. The title was passed on from one generation to the next. The Mirs possessed a broad autonomy between the Ottoman and Persian States. This autonomy varied from "Kurdish governments" to "independent sanjaks" (administrative districts) to "dependent sanjaks." In general, however, Kurdistan as a whole possessed a broad degree of autonomy in its internal structure. The aim of the Ottoman State was to do away with this autonomy as much as possible, thus incorporating the area fully into the empire. Continual warfare, exile, and execution led to the debilitation of the Kurdish ruling classes or Mirs. It is possible to follow some of these battles in the work *Letters on the Situation and Events in Turkey (1835-1839)* written by the German general Moltke while serving in the Ottoman Army.

The Mirs were done away with through long years of exile and confiscations of property. The vacuums they left behind were gradually filled by others, usually from their own close circles. These fresh replacements began to take the place of the Mirs who had come into confrontation with the Ottoman State and had either been exiled, executed, or killed in battle. By taking advantage of the conflict between the Mirs and the Ottoman State, the new leaders were able to increase their strength. This is how the Aghas came into being. Whereas the Mirs were a class based on the landed aristocracy, the Aghas' origins were in trade, farming, and livestock. The persons referred to as Aghas today were either farmers or petty traders on the Mirs' estates in the past. They raised livestock. The Aghas of today have a history going back no more than 160 years. The liquidation of the Mirs and the accompanying rise of the Aghas within the economic and social history of Kurdistan is highly significant.

The primary reason for founding a state known as Kurdistan within the borders of the Ottoman Empire in 1848 was to facilitate the destruction of Kurdistan's internal autonomous structure. This creation must be interpreted as an administrative measure towards the realization of the above stated goal. The Ottoman records show this state to have been on the books for some 20 years. The Ottoman Land Law of 1858 was passed with the same objective in mind—the full incorporation of Kurdistan into the empire.

The powers of the Aghas grew as that of the Mirs dwindled. The Ottoman State supported the Aghas against the Mirs, taking measures to bind them to the state. The Ottoman and Persian Empires were careful to apply the same policies in the area. Any forces capable of resisting were destroyed through war, execution, and exile. The new elements, which emerged in their places, were rendered dependent on the ruling state power. Once again the policy of divide and rule was enforced. A prime example is the establishment of the Hamidye cavalry in 1891. The latter were organized bands which stimulated conflicts amongst the Kurds themselves. The Hamidye cavalry units were comprised of Mirs who had chosen loyalty to the Ottoman state along with newly formed families of Aghas.

This process led to major changes in the class structure of Kurdistan and was finished off by the events of the 1940s, leading to the complete collapse of Kurdish ruling classes. The Agha families began to gain strength in the late nineteenth and early twentieth centuries. At the same time, there were Mir families waging a struggle against the Ottoman Empire. The Mir families are also referred to as dynasties.

These were the forces who fought for Kurdish national rights during the imperialist wars over Kurdistan and following the signing of the Lausanne Treaty which formalized the carving up of the Kurdish nation in the early twentieth century. Once the rebellions had been drowned in blood and all the centers of resistance broken up, the procedure we have outlined above was enforced, resulting in the success of the Turkish state. This was how agents were created. It is difficult to call these agents a Kurdish ruling class. Agents can never be rulers. Their primary function is to spread the official ideology and prevent Kurdish national development.

They assist the government in perpetrating exile, murder, torture, and genocide.

Sheikhs in the Service of the Official Ideology

In 1968 there was a Sheikh known as Sheikh Seyda living in Cizre. Sheikh Seyda tried to instill in his followers the belief that what mattered was to be a Muslim, a brother, a human being. "To nourish ethnic sentiments is contrary to Islam. God does not forgive those who do so. The Prophet Mohammed preached against taking in those who cherish their ethnicity, and we are his descendants..."

At that time an armed struggle was being waged between Kurds and the Iraqi government in Southern Kurdistan. The national liberation struggle being waged in the South had a great impact on the inhabitants of regions such as Hakkari, Siirt, Mardin, and Van, especially amongst the youth, some of whom sought ways to support the struggle. Moreover, major developments were occurring in the North as well. Herein lies the significance of the preaching of Sheikh Seyda to his followers. They were aimed at obstructing the arousal of national awareness. By stressing the importance of Islam, the national question faded out of the picture. Of course, "nourishment of ethnic sentiment" was only a sin when one happened to be a Kurd. None of the sheikhs had any objection against nourishing such sentiments if one was an Arab, Turk, or Persian.

A closer look shows us that Sheikh Seyda had close ties with the National Intelligence Agency (MIT). The Sheikh's preaching of Islamic internationalism was all in the service of propagating the official Turkish ideology and preventing the arousal of Kurdish national consciousness. Many sheikhs played such a role and were amply rewarded by the state. As the Turkish government's support enabled them to increase their economic power, they were likewise further able to increase their influence over the local population. They were granted generous bank credits, and provided with tractors, seed, and various kinds of commercial and agricultural credits. Whenever gas stations were opened, it was they who were granted the right of franchise.

When Sheikh Seyda died, his son Nurullah took his place. In contrast to his father, however, he did not do everything the government wished him to do. Several years ago he was killed in a mysterious traffic accident.

In an interview with Nadire Mater, İlhan Selçuk says the following about those members of Parliament who come from the East: "...After the transition to a multi-party regime, Ankara reached a compromise with the tribal heads and sheikhs. Tribal chiefs from the East and Southeast were directly incorporated into the multi-party regime. Not only did they never bring up the national issue of the people of the East, they never even mentioned democratic rights. Not a single parliamentary chief stood up in parliament to say, "Our people are oppressed, we want our democratic rights." Throughout the 1950s and up until the mid-1970s, the subject was never brought up.[9]

It is quite natural that none of the aghas, tribal chiefs, or sheikhs, either appointed or elected to parliament, ever demanded national rights. The reason they were in parliament in the first place was because they themselves denied their national identities and assisted in enforcing the policies of the Turkish government. The transition to a multi-party regime did not alter this state of affairs.

The Kemalists' main policy on Kurdistan was the annihilation and debilitation of all who came out in defence of national rights. This has remained the main policy of the state and has been faithfully applied by each successive government. One should examine this matter further to fully comprehend why various MPs who came from the East did not stand up and defend their own people and the regions they represented.

The position taken by the above mentioned collaborators cannot be comprehended without taking into account the Kemalist policy on Kurdistan. It is not possible to defend Kemalism and at the same time have a sound, scientific discussion regarding the economic, social and political elements of Kurdish society. It would be very difficult for Turkish intellectuals, who up till now have propagated Kemalism, to settle accounts on this matter. İlhan Selçuk's views on Kurdish rebellions are the same as those propounded by the official state ideology.

During the early years of the Turkish republic, government officials, members of the press, and other writers referred to Kurds as a primitive herd, "a horde which had not grasped humanity" led by shepherds and hodjas who were their exploiters. As an official state intellectual, Behçet Cemal, explains, "...Kurdish propaganda was initiated during the period of the Ottoman Tanzimat reforms after 1834, but it never made its way down to the people. This was because the changes that these laws would have brought about would have broken up the power and influence held by the aghas, sheikhs, chiefs, and hodjas over these primitive herds. There was no way to inculcate Kurdism into such a horde which had not yet grasped humanity. This horde, which considered existence to be nothing beyond a handful of millet and a handful of barley, knew nothing of what a republic was, or even what lay on the other side of the mountain they happened to live on—nor did they have any desire to know. Religious propaganda was what was required to stir up these masses, practically all of whom were lacking any knowledge of the outside world, and in reality, that is what was done.[10]

Obviously there were sheikhs, chiefs, and aghas with national sentiments who struggled for the Kurdish national movement, even though the above writer would have us believe the opposite. Such Kurds were bitterly attacked by the government, as well as by the press and other writers. It is today that the sheikhs have turned into agents and work for the government. A comparison of the authorities, writers, and the press' position concerning the events of the 1920s with those of the 1980s should certainly give us a clue regarding the nature of the political and social order in Turkey today.

The Eastern Trials of 1971

The events which took place in Diyarbekir during the Eastern Trials of 1971 are worthy of further comment. In those years, prisoners were allowed to receive visitors once a week. The visits took place in the open with the prisoners separated from their visitors by barbed wire. If there were only a few visitors, they were allowed longer visits. Everyone could talk with each others' visitors. Following some of the discussions which took place, I would hear such as the following: "So and so's father works for MIT... So and so's uncle is involved with MIT..." Some prisoners disclosed such information about those who came to see them.

Such connections should give rise neither to boasting nor to shame. They are objective facts. Many of the people who were influential in the democratic and revolutionary movement developing in Northern Kurdistan in the 1960s were the younger generation of the landowning classes. They were definitely opposed to the kinds of relationships their fathers and grandfathers had formed with the Turkish state. These developments led to harsh conflicts and friction inside numerous families.

In the 1971 trials of the Revolutionary Cultural Associations of the East, a very important incident occurred. The indictments prepared by the military attorneys stated that no nation known as Kurds had ever existed in history, that Kurds were actually Turks, while their language was a dialect of Turkish. It was emphasized that for the accused to claim they were Kurds was a crime. The military courts passed sentence based on these indictments, which were then approved by the military Supreme Court, and the claim that Kurds were actually Turks became official.

Some of the younger members of the Revolutionary Cultural Associations of the East who were on trial wished to reply to these indictments. In their reply, these youngsters pointed out that while the Turks had come to Anatolia from Central Asia in the eleventh century, Kurds were native to the area and had resided there since antiquity. The Kurds were also a separate nation whose language, history, culture, traditions, and customs were distinct from those of the Turks. The Turks were a Turanian people while the Kurds were Aryan.

The indictments prepared by the military attorneys said that Kurdish was not a distinct language, but consisted of a vocabulary that was 40% Turkish, 30% Arabic, 28% Persian, and the rest derived from various languages such as Armenian, Georgian, and Syriac. In their "Reply to the Indictment" the accused youths pointed out that such claims were unfounded and lacked serious content. They explained that Kurdish was distinct from Turkish in grammar, syntax, and phonetics. Turkish belongs to the Ural-Altaic language family, while Kurdish to Indo-European.

The "Reply to the Indictment" was prepared with great care and thoroughness in the summer of 1971 inside the Martial Law jail. Everyone in the prison was inspired by their enthusiasm. Most of the work was carried out in the canteen with all the parties working until late hours each night. Informers passed word of what was going on to the prison administration, who then tried to obstruct the work. Books and magazines needed for the preparation of the report were not allowed inside the prison. The dormitory cells were frequently searched, and the administration tried to get its hands on the work in progress. In spite of all this, the preparation of the "Reply to the Indictment" continued without interruption. Eventually, however, families began to act as obstacles to the work's completion. In the end, the MIT got involved.

On visitors' day, the various relatives of the prisoners would come and try to persuade the youths to give up the idea of preparing such a defence, while the prisoners would argue about the necessity to defend one's Kurdish identity. These arguments went on from week to week, with anxious families doing all they could to convince the prisoners to change their minds, or at least not to put their own names on such a project. The youths tried to reason with them, and criticized their fathers and uncles for their attitudes, telling them they had never done anything for the Kurds in the past but bow their heads and submit to enslavement. The latter answered saying, "You're right, we understand you, but sometimes you have to submit, you have to put up with things, we're powerless, what can we do?"

From time to time esteemed family members who had risen high in the state bureaucracy appeared at visiting hours. They tried to persuade the youths that such differences were of no consequence: they were all Muslims, they should enjoy their youth and not worry about such things, they should say whatever the prosecutors wanted them to say. The pressure mounted over time. The youths were even offered bribes. Their parents told them to forget about such nonsense and promised they would buy them cars, houses or whatever they wanted. The youths tried to reason with them, explaining that such bribes were no solution.

In one visit the youths were told that their proposed defence, rather than acting for the Kurds' welfare, would provoke the angry authorities into bombing Kurdish villages and similar catastrophes.

In spite of all opposition, a 167 page petition was prepared and signed. Later on, another 26 page petition was prepared and signed by other prisoners who were also tried for belonging to the Revolutionary Cultural Associations of the East.[11]

What I want to point out here was not the circumstances under which the petition was prepared, but the contact which the prison administration made with the prisoners' relatives. The prison authorities were able to bring individual families to pressure prisoners regarding what they should and should not do. The influence of the families was of no little consequence. It would be wrong to say that they were unable to influence their children in any way. For instance, some of the youths, rather than signing the 167 page petition they had prepared, wrote a separate 26 page petition of their own. However, due to the pressures from both their families and the courts, these petitions were never formally submitted. Nor were they able to disclose what they had written when they gave their statements in court.

But the presentation of the 167 page "Reply to the Indictment" to the courts gave rise to events of no little importance. The martial law authorities were opposed to placing a document which defended the Kurdish language and Kurdish identity in the court files because in that way the document would become official and could be used in the future. For this reason the court authorities refused to take the document and place it in their files. Instead they told the accused to present oral defences which would then be recorded. In reality very little of what was said was recorded. The Martial Law courts operated like branches of the national intelligence agency. For this reason the question of which documents were placed in the court's files and which were not was a political rather than a legal matter.

The youth on trial resisted, insisting that if their 'Reply to the Indictment' was not placed in the files, they would refuse to give statements. In this way they surprised all the Martial Law authorities, who expected them to say they were wrong, that they were also Turks, and that they wished to be forgiven. This was the kind of statement officials wished to place in the court files. The court tried to prevent recording the attitude and behavior of the youth in the trial records because that could serve as a source of moral support and strength for future generations. Following a long struggle, however, the court was forced to accept the 167 page document.

After the document was placed in the files and recorded in the minutes, the struggle entered a new phase. The accused wished to read the document along with their own testimonies at the trials. The court was against this under the pretext that it was too long and that they could read it themselves. These struggles lasted for months in late 1971 and early 1972. In the end, the text was read.

These trials had a great impact on the Martial Law authorities, who wanted the youth to say, "I never said I was a Kurd" or that the Kurds were a separate nation, or "I never encouraged anyone to speak Kurdish." The fact that the accused defended their "crimes" consciously, knowledgeably, and systematically led the authorities to lose confidence in the Turkish security establishment and bring in military personnel to assume internal security duties, while continuing to make use of local civilian officials at certain levels.

The most important elements of the 1971 Eastern Trials was that Kurds defended their own identities. The Kurdish defendants in similar trials following the 12 September coup were even more conscious and determined. All the arrested and accused spoke in Kurdish throughout the duration of trials. Even those who spoke and wrote Turkish well presented their defences in their own native language—Kurdish.

Given numerous obstacles, it is not easy to present one's defence in Kurdish. Every time the accused insist on speaking Kurdish they are committing an offence. The practice of speaking Kurdish is widespread in prisons and courtrooms all over the country today. Even though the state prosecutors understand nothing of what is being said, they continue to write the indictments in the same way as they always have done in the past. There are still hundreds of people standing trial just for speaking Kurdish, one of whom is Mehdi Zana, the former Mayor of Diyarbekir.

In response to Mehdi Zana's insistence on speaking Kurdish, Military Prosecutor Vedat Erkan stated that there was no such language as Kurdish in the Turkish state. In his words, "Kurdish is not a language. It is a heap of words. It is a restricted mass of words from words of pure Turkish origin which developed from ancient Turkish. Spoken by an insignificant number and encouraged by hostile forces outside the nation, calling this Kurdish is no indication that a separate Kurdish race and Kurdish language exists among the Turkish citizens living on Turkish soil. This is spoken in the East and Southeast today. As long as it is not used for purposes of propaganda or praise, and as long as there is no activity towards its use as a native language, or its broadcasting, or publication, there is no opposition. This is the truth. Deviation from the truth, however, and reference to people who do not know Turkish as Kurds and the dialect they speak as Kurdish is nothing more than a flagrant attempt to weaken patriotic sentiments." (*Cumhuriyet*, 11 August 1988).

The testimonies of those who speak Kurdish are recorded through the use of interpreters. How are these interpreters to have learned Kurdish? Normally, the courts require interpreters to have certification, such as university diplomas in the language they interpret. Can anyone who speaks Kurdish be considered a certified interpreter? Should they not have diplomas in Kurdish language and literature?

Two Major Fields of Activity of Military Courts

An important discussion has been going on since 1930. Should roads, schools, and water pipes be build in the East, or will that only accelerate the awakening of national sentiments? Because of fear for the latter, no investment or development was carried out throughout the years of single party rule. From 1950 onwards, roads, schools, and other social services began to be introduced, accompanied by the application of assimilation policies to prevent any Kurdish national awakening.

In fact, these assimilation policies have always been enforced, although we can see that they are more rigorously enforced in the aftermath of military coups. In Turkey, every time there is a military coup, two subjects are brought to the forefront. One is land reform, and the other is the intensification of the assimilation process. The desire for land reform is actually based on the misconception that it is the aghas who are inciting and provoking the national movement. According to this mentality, Kurdish identity can be eradicated at its source by exiling the aghas and confiscating their land. Following the military coup of 27 May 1960, the subject of land reform was widely debated by the universities, periodical press, and political parties.

Around that time, the Kurdistan Democratic Party under the leadership of Mullah Mustafa Barzani had commenced a struggle for national liberation in Southern Kurdistan, a fact which created great anxiety amongst the members of the National Unity Committee of Turkey. The struggle in the south had an impact on areas such as Hakkari, Van, Siirt, Mardin, and Diyarbekir, where there were efforts to collect aid for the struggle. Mullah Mustafa Barzani was known to be a landowner (agha), tribal chief, and sheikh. Due to the fear that similar activities would soon spread to the north, 485 aghas, sheiks, and tribal chiefs were rounded up and imprisoned in a camp in Sivas. A number of them were cruelly tortured, some had their teeth broken, and others were put into cesspools up to their necks. Fifty-five of them, who were considered exceptionally dangerous, were banished to non-Kurdish areas in the west of Turkey. All of these aghas, sheiks, and tribal chiefs were also subsequently followed upon their release or exile. Their ideas, contacts, life-styles, and activities were documented in great detail.

Meanwhile, it became clear that these were not the people behind the Kurdish movement. It was even observed that they had played influential roles in the spread of state propaganda. Thus, rather than being exiled and having their lands confiscated, it was suggested they should be encouraged to block the development of the Kurdish national movement more effectively. It was concluded that they should not be threatened with land reform, and those who had been exiled were soon "pardoned" and allowed to return home.

It was the young Kemalist officers who were primarily responsible for bringing up the issue of land reform after 27 May 1960. They were also partly motivated by a desire to help poor and landless peasants. Once it was understood, however, that the aghas, sheikhs, and tribal chiefs were on the side of the state, the question of land reform gradually faded away.

There are, in fact, some aghas, sheiks, and tribal chiefs who have taken part in the national liberation movement, but they are very few in number. The state is able to intervene and crush their influence quite easily. Since such persons are constantly in confrontation with the state, their property and wealth is always being threatened.

Amongst the 55 aghas mentioned above were some very intelligent minded landowners. Faik Buçak was one of these. In addition, there were also sheikhs, aghas, and tribal chiefs who took part in the Turkish Worker's Party founded in the early 1960s. Some were even elected to local government posts. A number of these were also active in the Eastern Demonstrations in 1967. They consciously and consistently defended their Kurdish identity. With the advancement of capitalist development in the late 1960s, however, some of them were assimilated and others even began to enforce assimilation mercilessly themselves. The advancement of capitalist relations without the presence of strong centers of opposition to conduct the ideological and political defence of the Kurdish national movement caused the destruction of some national values. However, today, due to the existence of strong elements defending Kurdish national values, the development of capitalism is not having the same destructive influence. We will go into this matter in more detail further on in this work.

The question of land reform in relation to the Kurdish issue was brought up again following the coup of 12 March 1971. This time, however, the debates did not last very long. The true identities of the landowners, sheikhs, and tribal chiefs and their function in the service of the state was soon unmasked. There were also attempts at forming a common front against the Kurdish national movement comprised of Turkish youths, intellectuals, and the press.

In the late 1960s the Kurdish question was the subject of a hot debate amongst revolutionary and democratic youths. The number of persons in favor of a democratic solution gradually increased. One of the aims of the 12 March junta was to halt these developments and disperse the existing organizations. By spreading the word that it was reactionary forces such as the aghas, sheikhs, and tribal chiefs who were behind the Kurdish issue, it was hoped that the youth would not lend the movement their support. Such state propaganda was supposed to draw attention away from the masses of poor peasants, although it was they who were mostly involved in the struggle.

There was also an economic dimension to land reform as it was brought up by the regime of 12 March. The developing industries of western Turkey needed markets. It was thought that land reform would increase the buying power of the people of the East and enable them to absorb some of the industrial products of the West.

Following the coup of 12 September 1980, the subject of land reform was on the agenda once again. This time, however, it was not linked to the Kurdish issue, nor did it last very long. As mentioned above, it was mainly brought up for economic purposes.

The second issue which is always brought up following each military coups is assimilation. How can Kurdish children be taught Turkish more effectively? What must be done to destroy Kurdish identity and have everyone shouting "How happy I am to be a Turk!"? This question was the subject of a loud and enthusiastic debate in the press and universities all over Turkey in the 1960s.

In 1960, Mehmet Sherif Fırat's book, *Doğu İlleri ve Varto Tarihi* was reprinted and distributed. This was another one of the books which claimed that there were no such people as Kurds, who were really Turks, and that Kurdish was a dialect of Turkish. Originally written in 1948, the 1960 reprint was widely distributed free of charge by the Ministry of Education to universities, professors, student associations, journalists, writers, and school libraries.

During this same period, numerous articles appeared stating that the Kurds were Turks. Language experts bent over backwards trying to prove that Kurdish was a variant of Turkish. University professors lent all their efforts to the task. Numerous seminars and conferences were held.

Throughout the 1960s, while the Kurdish movement was represented as reactionary effort under the control of landowners, it was considered a patriotic duty to prove that Kurds were Turks. Turkish teachers were assigned to teach in the East, and even those who considered themselves revolutionaries took leading roles in fulfilling their duties.

It was only towards the late sixties that such views began to be criticized. The rejection of these views first spread amongst Kurdish and later amongst Turkish revolutionaries. This process was further accelerated in the Eastern Demonstrations, which took place in various provinces in Kurdistan in the summer of 1967, and the founding of the Revolutionary Cultural Associations of the East. The founding of the Democratic Party of Kurdistan in Turkey in 1965 helped to straighten things up in rural areas. By the end of the sixties revolutionaries and democrats had firmly rejected the view that Kurds were really Turks. "Shoulder to shoulder in the fight against imperialism!" was a common slogan. That is how things were by 12 March 1971. The right wing in Turkey, however, in all its variants—radical, Islamic fundamentalist, Turkish racists, liberals—continue to maintain that Kurds are really Turks and the Kurdish language is an offshoot of Turkish.

The chief vehicles for assimilation have been the mass media and educational institutions. Every possible avenue has been tried to increase the influence of Turkish teaching in Kurdistan. From the early 1960s on, Regional Boarding Schools (*Bölge Yatılı İlkokullar*) began to be constructed in various regions of Kurdistan. Children who had reached primary school age were brought from their homes to study in an environment away from their families and villages. Such environments were conducive to assimilation because the children were permeated with Turkish language and ideology and had no contact with their native Kurdish culture whatsoever.

This technique was in fact quite similar to the old Ottoman practice of selecting boys—primarily Christian boys from the Balkans—and bringing them to study in the Sultan's schools where they were completely inculcated with a Turkish identity and the Muslim religion. All ties with their families were severed and the boys remained in the service of the Sultan.

In the Regional Boarding Primary Schools, children were forbidden to discuss their families and where they came from. Parents were allowed to speak only with their own children on visits and were not permitted to even ask the names of other students. In some cases students only found out, after they had graduated, that their good school friends were also their relatives! The schools were kept under strict discipline. During the regimes of 12 March and 12 September, military officers were appointed as headmasters. The aim of all these measures was to ensure the full severance of individuals from their Kurdish environment. Following the coup of 12 September 1980, assimilation was once again placed on the agenda, but this time without the earlier enthusiasm and fanfare. The task was left up to groups of experts rather than made the subject of public debates and seminars. This change was due to the fact that the official ideology was widely criticized and more and more people were calling for a democratic solution to the Kurdish problem. The government did not want to provoke discussion on the issue because they were no longer so firmly in control.

Nevertheless, institutions such as the Turkish Cultural Research Institute (*Türk Kültürü Araştırma Enstitüsü*) and the Anatolian Press Agency (*Anadolu Basın Birliği*) have printed numerous publications asserting that Kurds are Turks and Kurdish is a dialect of Turkish. "Scientific meetings" have been organized on this subject throughout the country, especially in Kurdish cities, regional government offices, military headquarters, and universities. The literacy courses which were commenced following 12 September were meant for the assimilation of Kurds.

The Use of Islamist Ideology Against the Kurdish Question

In the 1973 general elections, the National Salvation Party (*Milli Selamet Partisi* or MSP) received 11.8% of votes nationwide. This figure was twice as high in Kurdish districts. In 1977, the general percentage of votes for the same party fell to only 3.3%, although its proportion had increased in Kurdistan. The only place in the East where MSP received less votes in

1977 was Erzurum, where the lost votes went over to the Nationalist Action Party (*Milliyetçi Hareket Partisi* or MHP).[12]

In the 1977 general elections, the Republican Peoples Party (*Cumhuriyet Halk Partisi* or CHP) registered an 8.1% increase in votes when compared to 1973 on a nation wide scale, but this percentage fell in some parts of Kurdistan. The National Salvation Party, which received 3.3% less than in 1973, registered major gains in Kurdistan. The same held for the Prosperity Party (*Refah Partisi* or RP), its successor, which received 20% of the vote in Kurdistan in the 1987 general elections, although the nationwide average was 7.8%. This party had its basis in Islamic ideology, which gave it great utility in the service of the official ideology. Even though the government has occasionally charged the Prosperity Party with being anti-Kemalist, the secret services have actually encouraged the growth of such a party.

Following the coup of 12 March 1971, the Constitutional Court, banned the National Order Party (*Milli Nizam Partisi* or MNP) along with the Turkish Workers Party (*Türkiye İşçi Partisi* or TIP). Once it was realized, however, that an Islamic based party was necessary for retarding the growth of the Kurdish national movement, the same military officials, who had banned the MNP, encouraged the leaders of that party to return back to the country from exile. Upon their return a new party was formed and given the name National Salvation Party (*Milli Selamet Partisi* or MSP).

In 1962 an American professor by the name of Frey carried out a survey in Turkey in conjunction with the Bureau of Research and Testing at the Ministry of Education and the Agency for International Development (AID).[13] Although the results of the survey were published in the United States, the Turkish government attempted to prevent these results from reaching the Turkish public. In spite of these efforts, several articles were published on the subject.[14] It became clear from the information provided at the end of the research project, that American government officials were proposing that the best way for the Turkish government to fight against the spread of the Kurdish struggle was through the creation and institutionalization of a party based on religion. The proposal prepared by American Peace Corps volunteers was taken seriously and from that date on, the friction between the Turkish government and Kurdish sheikhs was reduced to a minimum.

There are two other points one should note in this matter. Today one cannot say that all Kurdish sheikhs are anti-Kurdish and cooperating with the Turkish secret services. There are some who still struggle for Kurdish rights, although they are generally weak and their influence is waning. On the other hand, those sheikhs who receive privileges and financial rewards from the state, also increase their wealth and influence amongst the people. The latter sheikhs are constantly making anti-Kurdish propaganda by calling supporters of the Kurdish liberation movement infidels, communists, and traitors. Prior to 1980, not only the National Salvation Party, but also the Justice Party, National Action Party, and Republican People's Party used this sort of propaganda. Most of the sheikhs who are active in these parties are related through family ties. As MPs, senators, and in other positions of power, they claim "national volition" when furthering the colonialists' control over Kurdistan.

The preservation of the traditional status-quo in Kurdistan is seen as essential to prevent the spread of Kurdish democratic and national rights. For this reason the institution of sheikhs will not be done away with, either in Turkey or in any other states colonizing Kurdistan.

Kamran Inan is a sheikh who is proud to spread Turkish propaganda. He is the type who, upon hearing that some Turk in Bulgaria has a nosebleed, would submit a resolution to the European Parliament denouncing the oppression of Turks in that country. He is always fraught with anxiety over the future of the Turks in Kerkuk (Iraq), Western Thrace (Greece), and Cyprus, and he jumps at the opportunity to broach the subject. He never opens his mouth, when it comes to the oppression of Kurds. He pretends to be unaware of even the most flagrant violations of human rights, including violations such as the genocide of over 5,000 Kurds in Halabja (Iraq) in 1988. He is always high up in the ranks of whatever party is in power (or is expected to come into power). Needless to say, the Turkish government has a great need for men such as him.

Let's take another look back at June 1987, when the Bulgarian government began sending members of the Bulgarian Turkish minority to Turkey. By August over 300,000 people had crossed the border and the Turkish government was forced to close the border. The fact that these Bulgarian Turks were only allowed to bring a small amount of cash and goods with them gave rise to protests by the Turkish authorities, who did everything they could to bring the matter to the attention of the West. Turkish politicians, the media, the trade union confederation, etc. severely criticized European governments and the western public for not showing sufficient interest in the fate of Bulgarian Turks. Kamran Inan held a press conference in Paris where he denounced western governments and human rights associations, accusing them of applying double standards in human rights.

However, also in the first week of June 1989, there were reported cases of poisoning in the Kurdish refugee camps in Kiziltepe. The refugees stated that the bread they were fed had been injected with chemical substances, one of which was rat poison. To ensure success, the poison had been injected after the bread was cooked, since cooking could have reduced the effects of the poison! The refugees charged that this event had been organized by the Iraqi secret services in conjunction with the Turkish secret services.[15]

After these events leaked to the press, the Turkish authorities prohibited entrance into the refugee camp, and refugees were forbidden to go shopping in Kiziltepe and Mardin. Government authorities denied the truth of the reported events. Official statements simply retorted that "following an examination, no traces of illness were found." (*Tercüman*, 10 June 1989). The Iraqi ambassador in Ankara, Abduljabbar Jevad, accused Barzani of poisoning the Kurds in the camp as well as perpetrating the massacre in Halabja (*Milliyet*, 27 June 1989).

Meanwhile, also in June 1989, the racist, colonialist, and fascist administration in Southern Kurdistan continued to burn Kurdish villages and towns, force people to leave their homes for the desert, and round up Kurds into concentration camps.

Therefore, the timing of the poisoning incident in the Kiziltepe camp took place just at that moment that Bulgarian Turks were pouring into Turkey and were being welcomed with open arms. Kamran Inan was busy denouncing "Bulgarian tyranny" to the west while he remained silent over the tyranny faced by Iraqi Kurds or the attempts at poisoning other Kurds in the Kiziltepe refugee camp in Turkey. Kamran Inan is exactly the type of "Eastern Citizen" sought by the Turkish government. Without a doubt, Inan's remarkable capacity to overlook even the most flagrant infringements of human rights in Kurdistan has allowed him to reach the upper echelons of the Turkish state bureaucracy.

The Meaning of Turk/Islam Synthesis From the Point of View of the Kurdish Issue

The Turk-Islam synthesis is one of the current variants of the official state ideology. At the moment it has become difficult to continue the propaganda based on the concept of Turkish superiority. Consequently, there has been a shift in emphasis and it is now the concept of Islam which is stressed. In my opinion the spread of this variant of the official ideology is primarily aimed at the Kurdish districts. For instance, the Guidance

Team formed by the Department of Religious Affairs in 1984 has been busy giving sermons in all Kurdish villages, towns, coffeehouses, mosques, schools, and military bases in which both Islam and Ataturk's political doctrines are preached. The deeds of the PKK are referred to as violations of both the principles Islam and humanity. The local population is called upon to join in the struggle against the PKK.

Similar propaganda is being spread in universities. Many views similar to those mentioned above are expressed by university professors throughout these same regions.[16]

One newspaper article in *Hürriyet* (21 April 1987) entitled "Religious Officials Have Been Appointed to 17 Provinces" described the situation as follows:

> 17 guidance (enlightenment) teams comprised of religious officials are on duty in various provinces. Along with working at the mosques, these teams also hold religious discussions and question and answer sessions in secondary schools, universities, and army barracks.
>
> Members of the "Guidance Teams" attend intensive seminars given by the MIT and Police Headquarters prior to their "assignments." Each team is composed of 2-3 religious officials.
>
> The 17 provinces where teams have been assigned are: 1) Tekirdağ-Kirklareli; 2) Ağrı-Kars; 3) Erzurum-Erzincan; 4) Van-Hakkari; 5) Siirt-Muş-Bitlis; 6) Mardin-Diyarbekir; 7) Bingöl-Tunceli; 8) Adıyaman-Şanlıurfa.

Another article in *Hürriyet* (21 April 1987) related as follows:

> Van 100 Year University President, Prof. Dr. Nihat Baysun: No Sermon was Preached at our University; A Conference was held on Unity and Togetherness
>
> The conference was jointly organized by the governor's office in Diyarbekir, Dicle University, and the high committee on Ataturk, Culture, Language, and History.
>
> The following professors were participating in the conference, which will also be held in other Eastern provinces such as Gaziantep, Şanlıurfa, Malatya and Kahramanmaraş: Prof. Dr. Bahaeddin Ögel, Associate Prof.

Dr. Coşkun Alptekin, Associate Prof. Dr. Abdülhalik Çay, Assistant Associate Prof. Dr. İlhan Sahin.

The fact that all the countries which colonize Kurdistan are of the same religion gives rise to major misconceptions. The cause of "religious fraternity" is employed to frustrate the desires and goals of the Kurdish movement. The colonialist states have also resorted to stirring up historical differences such as those between Alevis and Sunnis to conceal the fact that there is a national question at play.

The objective is to use religious ideology as a check on the development of the Kurdish national movement. This is certainly not the first time in history that religious sentiments have been employed against the development of a national liberation movement. In the late nineteenth century, for example, the El-Mehdi movement in Sudan, which was presented as a religious movement, was actually a rebellion of the Sudanese against British imperialism. The same can be said for the Omer Mukhtar movement in Libya during the time of Mussolini's rule, which was a rebellion against Italian imperialism under a religious guise.

The Turk-Islam synthesis is obviously tightly related to the advancement of the armed struggle in Kurdistan. Leaflets urging the local population to fight against the PKK are distributed from planes and helicopters. The message contained in these leaflets states: "The PKK has its eyes on your wives, your daughters, and your honor. You are Muslims. You have no other thought but to be good Muslims. Our government safeguards Islam. This is why we need your help in the fight against these bandits and perverts." Obviously only the state can be behind the distribution of such leaflets by air.

One of the most important effects of the advancement of the guerrilla struggle in Kurdistan has been the questions and debates it has engendered. People have begun to ask themselves why there are parts of Kurdistan in Turkey, Iraq, Iran and Syria; why Kurdistan had been divided; why Kurdistan has been the object of a policy of divide and rule, etc. By calling the guerrillas "traitors to the infidels... bandits... cowards..." and so on, the government is hoping to curb the spread and intensification of these debates.[17]

Considering that similar problems are not present in the Aegean and Central Anatolian regions, no one has felt the need to send Guidance Teams to these areas, nor to distribute leaflets by helicopters.

The Results of the Breakdown of the Class Basis of Nationalistic Ideas

The fact that the landowners, sheikhs, and tribal chiefs of Kurdistan were made into agents is closely related to the failure of the development and spread of Kurdish nationalistic ideas. The transformation of the Kurdish ruling class into an agent class has meant the breakdown of the class which could have supported, strengthened, and spread nationalistic ideas. Were Kurdish society to live out its own history, without the break up of its own inner dynamics due to outside factors, a Kurdish bourgeoisie could have emerged with its own identity, and capitalist development could have taken place in a clearer fashion. The landed aristocracy could have developed into a bourgeoisie. Such a process would have safeguarded a Kurdish ethnic identity. Bourgeoisie classes of other nations do not deny their own identities while entering into international relations. Neither the Turkish nor the Arab bourgeoisies deny their own identities in their dealings with imperialism.

Not a Ruling Class But an Agent Class

There have been three major policy directives enforced in Kurdistan since the 1940s (1) Efforts designed to turn the Kurdish landowning aghas, sheikhs, and tribal chiefs into agents of the state; (2) Policies to keep feudal institutions alive to deform capitalist development as far as possible; (3) Transferring any capital amassed in the East, however small, to the western part of Turkey. All investments in the East were to be carried out through the state. Turkish capital may have flown from the west to the east, but no capital of Kurdish origin was to be invested in the area.

Several groups of the Turkish left espouse the view that Turkey is ruled by joint Turkish and Kurdish ruling classes and that there is no longer a national bourgeoisie but one that collaborates with imperialism. The view that a joint Turkish and Kurdish bourgeoisie hold sway over Turkey is a blatant lie. Kurdish landowners who take part in the ruling class do so not as Kurds but because they identify completely with the ideology of the Turkish state. They are accepted into Turkish ruling circles because they have assumed duties as regional agents for the Turkish state.

What are the policies of the Turkish bourgeoisie when it comes to social and cultural matters? When we look a bit deeper into the issue we see that the state, along with many private corporations and banks, rewards those who further Turkish poetry, literature, music, art, and athletics in all sorts of ways. The Turkish bourgeoisie will always take care to encourage the development of a Turkish language, culture, educational system, and research into social and political relations, no matter what sort of relations they maintain with wider imperialist circles.

Has anyone ever heard of any Kurds being rewarded for their beautiful literary works, or their fine use of the Kurdish language? Are there any industrialists or big business people known for their defence of Kurds? Are there any incentives given to the advancement of Kurdish culture, music, art, and theatre? Where is the supposed Kurdish bourgeoisie to encourage the spread and development of Kurdish culture? We all know the repression faced by decent people or revolutionaries who wish to speak and write in Kurdish. As for the powerful sheikhs, aghas, and tribal chiefs, not only do they not reward those who contribute to the development of Kurdish language and culture, they even fight against anyone who voices demands related to this matter. They turn them over to the state authorities! That is exactly why they have been welcomed by the state in the first place. Such people can certainly not be called part of a Kurdish ruling class. They are simply agents. While objectively they are Kurds, subjectively they are Turks. In this case, how can anyone say that Turkey is ruled by the Turkish and Kurdish ruling classes together?

In my opinion, no politician, writer, or artist of Kurdish origin who does not emphasize his Kurdishness, who does not write, create, or participate in politics *as a Kurd* is worthy of being called a *Kurdish* writer, artist, or politician.

The thesis that the bourgeoisie today has lost its national characteristics and has been transformed into a collaborationist class can not be used to explain the identification of the Kurdish landowning sectors, tribal chiefs, businessmen, and industrialists with the Turkish ruling classes. When we say that the bourgeoisie today has lost its national characteristics, we mean that the bourgeoisie does not put forth the interests of the nation above all, but invites the imperialists to exploit their country. Nevertheless, neither the Turkish nor any other national bourgeoisie, such as the Arab or Persian ones, do so on the basis of refuting their own national identities. The Kurdish landowners not only do everything possible to facilitate the exploitation of Kurdistan by the Turkish bourgeoisie, they even go so far as to give up their national identities to become one with the latter.

The social and political situation we have outlined above is of no minor consequence. This process of denial lends Kurdish society its own distinctive structure and peculiarities. From this perspective, there is no other society in the world resembling Kurdish society in Turkey.

In spite of all that we have just described, the Turkish security forces still go to great lengths to prepare reports on pro-government versus anti-government landlords. This just goes to show that no matter the degree to which Kurds turn into agents, the Turkish state still distrusts them.

According to a 1969 "top secret report" prepared by the Ministry of the Interior—and used as proof in accusations against certain aghas—tribal chiefs can be divided chronologically into two separate categories.[18] The first group includes landowners, sheikhs, and tribal chiefs who took part in developing the Kurdish national movement between 1925-1938. As we know, these individuals were dealt with in various means, including interrogation, torture, execution, exile, armed assaults, and so on.

A few of these sheikhs, tribal chiefs, and landlords, who had participated in uprisings during this period, saved their necks by bribery and co-optation to support the Turkish state thereafter. However, once the rebellions had been put down, they were sent into exile along with others who had participated in the Kurdish movement.

It can be stated that, prior to the Turkish Republic, the predominant means of production and social relations in Kurdish society was feudal. Villages and tribes were self-sufficient with no need of the outside world. Consequently, it was very difficult for imperialists and colonialists to exercise complete control over such a society. A significant portion of the landowners, sheikhs, and tribal chiefs possessed patriotic sentiments. They opened medresses (theological schools attached to mosques) where education was in Kurdish. In addition, there were persons, known as *dengbej*, who sang, told stories, and sometimes performed circus acts. The living expenses of these persons were covered by the aghas, lords, sheikhs, and chiefs. They were an important factor in the transmission of Kurdish language and literature through the ages. Many of them assumed leadership roles in Kurdish movements during the Ottoman period as well as in the early years of the Republic.

The second group identified in the Ministry of Interior's secret report included aghas, sheikhs, and tribal chiefs who were co-opted by the Turkish government from the 1940s onwards. However, the PKK's raids in Eruh and Shemdinli in 1984 brought about a fundamental change in the Kurdish movement in Turkey.

Those sectors of Kurdish society, who deny their own identity and propagandize the views of the Turkish state as agents against the Kurdish national movement can not be referred to as a "Kurdish bourgeoisie." Where on earth has a bourgeoisie of such a nature ever existed? Given the erosion of a Kurdish ruling class with nationalist sentiments today, it is democrats and revolutionaries who fight against the repression of the Kurdish language and culture.

There is also another dimension in the conscious destruction of the very structure of Kurdish society. One could argue that a movement in which large landowners, sheikhs, tribal chiefs, and businessmen do not participate is a democratic movement. Since all the above are actually against the movement, the Kurdish nationalist movement today is by definition a democratic one.

Kurdish revolutionaries now have an objective duty on their shoulders—the defence of the Kurdish language and culture, as well as other characteristics particular to Kurdish society. The majority within the Turkish left oppose the Kurdish nationalist struggle as a deviation. They do so in the name of internationalism and the working class, and claim that once socialism is established, national problems will be solved on their own. This attitude, which was especially prevalent prior to 1980, can still be heard in some circles today. Even though their position may appear correct at first, it is in fact very dangerous given the reality of Kurdistan. Their refusal to take a stand against the repression of the language and culture of an oppressed people only reinforces the thoughts and actions of the dominant classes. It strengthens the latter's morale. Constant repetition of the writings of Lenin and Stalin on the principle of the right of nations to self-determination does nothing to bring about a solution to a very concrete problem. Moreover, assimilation is an oppressive process which should never be approved under any circumstance.[19]

The Situation in Eastern and Southern Kurdistan

Clearly, the situation we have outlined above refers to Northern Kurdistan. In Eastern Kurdistan (Iran) and Southern Kurdistan (Iraq) things are a bit different. The policies aimed at turning Kurds in those countries into Persians or Arabs were unsuccessful. One of the primary reasons they were unable to achieve this in Iran was that taking the various ethnic groups as a whole—Azeri, Kurd, Turkmen, Baluci, Arabs etc.—the Persians actually constituted a minority in Iran. Iraq, on the other hand, was a British colony for many years, up until nearly the end of World War II. The British and French colonialists had no special policies aimed at destroying the ethnic identities of the nations they colonized. During the period when Iraq was a British colony, the Kurdish language was actually able to develop, though to a limited degree. Kurds also took advantage of every available opportunity to defend their national and democratic rights.

Consequently, they achieved important successes which made it difficult to deny their existence in Iraq.

In both of Iran and Iraq, landowners, sheikhs, and tribal chiefs loyal to the state are rewarded by various means and employed against those fighting for Kurdish national liberation. In Iraq such individuals have often been decorated with medals for their services after fighting alongside government forces against other Kurds. The government gives such Kurdish collaborators weapons and money. As a result, fighting often breaks out between Kurds who have government ties and Kurds who fight for national liberation.

However, one thing should be kept in mind about these relations. Those persons who enter into agreements with the Iraqi and Iranian governments as *Kurdish* landowners, tribal chiefs, sheikhs, and businessmen are always treated as subordinates. Jihangir Agha in Iran, and Abdullah Beshir Agha (Erbil area) in Iraq, for instance, maintained close relations with the regimes of Khomeini and Saddam Hussein in such capacities. This should not be interpreted to mean that these Kurdish aghas, tribal chiefs, sheikhs, and businessmen were in power on par with the Persian and Arab bourgeoisies. These states actually follow their policies of divide and rule by recognizing the Kurdish identities of their collaborators. They use "lionlike Kurds" against "Kurdish bandits" by giving the former all sorts of rewards, financial and otherwise. Of course there are still many landowners, sheikhs, and tribal chiefs, in both Iran and Iraq, who participate in the Kurdish national liberation movement. Those Kurds who fight against the Kurdish national movement do so because that way their own class interests are better protected by the state.

The Turkish Left and the Kurdish Question

Following the coup of 27 May 1960, a discussion of the Kurdish issue took place amongst the Turkish left. Even though the issue was originally taken up with as little challenge as possible to the basic tenets of Kemalism, this was still a significant beginning. The credit for bringing up the issue was primarily due to the presence of Kurdish revolutionaries within these leftist movements. In contrast, during the 1920s and 1930s the Turkish left had been entirely Kemalist in its approach to the Kurdish issue. One could even say it was hostile and anti-Kurd.

The second dimension of this discussion was the negative effect of the Turkish left on the development of the Kurdish national movement. First, it should be made clear, that Turkish nationalism and Kurdish nationalism are the product of two different social and political processes.

While Turks are a dominant nation, and reading and writing Turkish is encouraged and rewarded for all citizens of the Republic of Turkey, Kurds are an oppressed nation whose national and democratic rights have been usurped. For this and all the reasons we have given so far, democratically-minded and revolutionary people should defend Kurdish culture and its values. However, often, Kurdish leftists who defend such values are charged by Turkish leftists as being "nationalists" rather than revolutionaries. Many Kurdish revolutionaries have in fact been influenced by such arguments and, in the 1960s for instance, Kurdish leftists refrained from speaking Kurdish amongst themselves so that they would not be labelled as nationalists. They never openly expressed the fact that they were Kurds. They knocked themselves out to show that they were Marxist-Leninists, but tried to cover up any particular traits they might have due to their Kurdishness.

Prior to 1980 as well, people who took a stand against the repression of the Kurdish language and culture, or spoke Kurdish, or came out in favor of an independent Kurdish state were branded as "nationalists." Nationalism was rendered an abstract and hollow concept, with no distinction made between the nationalism of an oppressed nation and an oppressor nation. Alpaslan Türkeş and Molla Mustafa Barzani were lumped together in the same basket, without a distinction made between the two entirely different social and political phenomena they represented. Persons who stated that Kurdish should be allowed to be spoken freely were charged with "nationalism" while the racist, colonialist, and assimilationist policies of the Turkish state were supported. The slogan "For an independent Turkey!" was considered to be revolutionary, and the slogan "For an independent Kurdistan!" was labelled nationalist! The slogan "independent Turkey" signified the acceptance and approval of the imperialist war for the division of Kurdistan which was waged in the 1920s. Of course, the 1920s policy of divide and rule was a joint action between British imperialists and Kemalists, with the latter receiving a major share of Kurdistan.

The attitude of the Turkish left on the Kurdish issue is now worthy of careful examination. It is not enough to look at Turkey's problems only from the perspective of a class struggle. It must also be considered from the perspective of the ethnic factor. In reality, social and political institutions, treaties, and historical events mean different things for different ethnic groups. The ideas of Mihri Belli, one of the major Marxist-Leninist leaders in the history of the Turkish left, are an important example in this respect.

As a young man, Mihri Belli studied economics at a university in the United States of America. As soon as World War II broke out, he returned to Turkey and enlisted in the army. Mihri Belli considers the army to have been a progressive, revolutionary institution prior to the 1950s. He called for all communists and socialists to join the army to defend the country from a probable Nazi invasion. He often points out that at that time Turkey was not a NATO member, so that the pre-1950 army was not a NATO army, and Turkey was an independent and anti-imperialist state.[20]

A Turkish Marxist, then, is able to characterize the Turkish army in this way. No Kurdish Marxist would make this same characterization given the role played by the Turkish army in the repression of Kurdish uprisings during the formation of the Republic. The army was the perpetrator of nothing less than genocide in both the Zilan and Dersim regions. All the villages in the Zilan valley were burned and razed by planes and bombs, while their inhabitants were rounded up in camps and mowed down by firing squads. Such massacres were repeated over and over again in Dersim. Every possible form of state terror was applied to intimidate the Kurdish people and do away with their desire for democratic and national rights. Nevertheless, during the wars between the Turks, Greeks and Armenians, Turks promised the Kurds national rights to enlist support. The denial of the existence of a Kurdish nation began with the founding of the Turkish Republic.

History does not consist only of events which have been written down. Many events have taken place which do not appear in any books, and the vast majority of people are unaware of them. The fact that some events are played up by the press while others never reach print is influenced by official ideologies. This is clearly not a scientific approach to the study of the world.

What Hitler did to the Jews is known because it has been written down and thoroughly documented. On the other hand, there are no official records of the massacres of the Kurds repeatedly throughout history. If such records did exist, they have probably been destroyed, or perhaps they have been locked away somewhere to which there is no access. No researchers will ever be able to reach them.

What happened in Halabja in Southern Kurdistan in mid-March 1989 passed into the annals of history in spite of all repression and terror. Nevertheless, it should not be overlooked that in the autumn of 1988, the French government held an international conference for the restriction and gradual abolition of chemical warfare. As a nation which has been the target of intense chemical warfare, the Kurds wished to take part in the conference. However, states which have massacred and used chemical weapons against Kurds were vehemently opposed to Kurdish representation in this meeting. Even at a conference of this nature, the desires of states which have practiced genocide was adhered to, and the participation of Kurds was barred. This incident alone is an indication of the perilous state of human rights today.

Another example of the difference in perspectives between Turkish and Kurdish Marxists is their attitude to Shefik Hüsnü. He is another individual who is exalted by the Turkish left because he enlisted in the Turkish army during World War II. For Kurds, though, he is one more of their thousands of enemies. Shefik Hüsnü took the side of the Kemalists during Kurdish uprisings and applauded the massacres which followed. In fact, nothing could be worse for the Turkish left than to try and get Kurds to recognize Shefik Hüsnü as a great leader.

There was an interesting debate on this subject in the two magazines *Medya Güneşi* and *Özgür Gelecek* which followed a "Call for the Commemoration of Dr. Shefik Hüsnü Deymer on the 30th Anniversary of his Death" published in *Özgür Gelecek* (February 1989, no. 3). Sinan Doğru, writing in *Medya Güneşi*, pointed out that since Shefik Hüsnü joined his bourgeoisie in hostilities against Kurds, the latter should not participate in such a commemoration.[21]

Today, Ubeydullah Nehri, Alisher, Sheikh Said, Ihsan Nuri, Simko, Seyid Rıza, Qadi Mohammed, and Molla Mustafa Barzani are all major Kurdish patriots. Turkish nationalists, however, as well as the Turkish left, characterize them as British agents, brigands, bandits and so on.

The Concept of "Minority Racism"

Various politicians and newspaper columnists, including Prof. Turhan Feyzioğlu, Alpaslan Türkeş, İsmail Cem, Coşkun Kirca, Rauf Tamer, Uğur Mumcu, and Ergun Göze accuse Kurds of "minority racism." The journalist and writer, Uğur Mumcu, in an interview with Halil Berktay for *Saçak* magazine, stated the following points as "the three conditions for Turkish socialism": (1) the Turkish left must not become a tool for minority racism, *i.e.* Kurdism; (2) Kurdish socialists must emphasize their disagreement with adventurist currents at all times; (3) Turkish socialists must preserve their ideological independence.[22]

In essence, even as late as 1986, we see the Kurdish struggle against assimilation and colonialist practices characterized by the Turkish press as "minority racism." Turkish socialists are advised to stay out of the Kurdish issue. For Uğur Mumcu not to make even the slightest criticism of the racist and colonialist policies against Kurds by his own government, and for him to go so far as to characterize Kurdish desires for democratic and national rights as "minority racism," shows the true colors of that author.

Indeed, in an article on the situation of the Turkish minority in Greece, however, this same writer criticizes the assimilation policies applied by the Greek government, saying, "Basic rights and liberties cannot be said to differ from one country to the next. We should not simply sit back and say that it does not matter whether or not this or that society possesses such rights."[23] What could be more racist than considering that another nation is unworthy of what one considers one's own nation to be worthy of, and then applauding the plans designed to annihilate the Kurdish identity! Elsewhere, this same writer states, "The minority racism of yesterday, with its reactionary appearance with foreign support, can be expected to reappear today under a 'leftist' guise. Under this mask lies the same essence: foreign supported separatism and minority racism. The Turkish republic will crush this aggression and, without resorting to undemocratic methods, will extinguish any sort of terrorist activity. In order to do so, citizens against minority racism and every sort of terror must join hands and hearts in the struggle."[24]

Ismail Cem has expressed similar views in various articles, charging Kurds with "racism" while characterizing the policies of the Turkish state in Kurdistan as "modern." Of course these same writers applaud the Turks in Bulgaria for coming out against forced name changes and defending their Turkish identities.

Let's not forget the murder of over 40 revolutionaries and democratically minded individuals through torture in Diyarbekir prison in the aftermath of 12 September. They were killed for defending their Kurdish identities. Diyarbekir Military Prison was a living hell for both prisoners and their families. In spite of this, writers such as Uğur Mumcu and İsmail Cem did not raise even the slightest criticism against these racist, colonialist, and fascist policies which have yet to be surpassed in the world. They chose to remain silent, thus expressing their tacit approval. As for Kurds who call for national and democratic rights, they are characterized as "outdated."

Turkish writers often blame their failure to take up the Kurdish issue on laws, saying that there are restrictions against criticism of the official ideology. Although this argument is not without some basis, one can not overlook the fact that these same writers have actually identified with the antidemocratic practises to which Kurds are subjected. In my opinion, their support is a primary cause for the continuing state of affairs.[25] For example, in an article entitled "Milli Birlik Ortami," Coşkun Kirca writes that "the separatists eager for independence, or the dreamers of autonomy, will be damned into seeing that no one has any choice other than becoming a Turk or being absorbed into Turkhood." The same writer, in his article, "Diller ve Dilcikler," stresses the point that Kurdish is a primitive language, and that it would constitute great progress if it was uprooted. He says that assimilation is necessary and would be to the benefit of Kurds.[26]

There is another point that needs to be raised when discussing "minority racism." First of all, Kurds are not a minority. But even if they were, should they not make their existence known, and should they not defend "minority rights?" None of the above-mentioned writers has ever expressed an opinion on the usurped national and democratic rights of Kurds. When discussions come to such subjects, Turkish commentators generally keep their mouths shut, but when it comes to apportioning blame, there is no stopping them.

From August 1984 on, Turkish newspapers began devoting front page coverage to the fighting between the PKK and the Turkish security forces. What the newspapers did not reflect, although it was well known by the journalists who covered these conflicts, were the national and democratic demands raised by the Kurdish guerrillas in conjunction with attacks on Turkish security forces. In leaflets and brochures they distributed throughout their areas of operation, the guerrillas defended the rights of Kurdish communities along with other demands. They called for an end to the oppression of the Kurdish language and culture. The contents of these brochures, which had a very positive effect on the Kurdish people, were never revealed in the press, even though the journalists were very familiar with them. In my opinion, this omission was rooted in the fact that Turkish writers and journalists were opposed to the guerrillas' propaganda. Thus, they chose to ignore these aspects of the guerilla struggle and play up their fight with the state security forces.

This scorn and deprecation of Kurdish national sentiments and demands by Turkish leftists and social-democrats is of no little consequence. There is no doubt that one of the primary reasons prison authorities were able to torture and kill their charges with such ease was because they knew they would not be criticized for doing so. An administration which knew it would be criticized by the press and called to account would have hesitated before acting in such a criminal fashion. There seems to be an unspoken contract between the Turkish press and the regime of torture. Whatever the regime does in Kurdistan, the press will praise it.

At last the events of our time are causing Turkish writers and journalists to shift their views on this issue. A number of major changes are taking place, especially in the attitudes and actions of leftists, who have started to follow the policies of the Turkish government in Kurdistan more closely. The armed struggle, various events in prisons, and the mass influx of thousands of Turks from Bulgaria have forced journalists and writers to take a more serious approach to the Kurdish issue. The liberation of thought goes hand in hand with the questioning of the official ideology and the revelation of the true nature of the Kurdish question in Turkey.

The Significance of the Debate on the Mode of Production in Kurdistan

The question whether the predominant mode of production in Kurdistan is feudal or capitalist has led to a widespread debate. Since the development of the relations of production in one direction or another is not always determined by a particular society's internal dynamics, I do not believe that this debate is a productive one. Whether or not a society remains feudal or undergoes capitalist development may rest entirely on external factors. This is generally true in colonial societies, where the internal dynamics of indigenous groups have been shattered. Such societies no longer determine their own history, which, instead, becomes the product of outside interests. This situation is even more true where Kurdistan is concerned given the fact that the ruling class here has lost its identity altogether and turned into an agent class.

Under these conditions, the continuation of feudal relations of production is something determined by forces intervening from the outside. Had the internal dynamics of Kurdish society been stronger, external actors would not have been able to break up and paralyze this society, nor enforce economic, social, and cultural policies to serve the interests of imperialist states. Had the internal dynamics of Kurdish society been stronger, appropriate policies would have come into play in accordance with the needs of the Kurdish nation. Thus, the mode of production should only be discussed after establishing these parameters of discussion. In this way it will become clearer why productive relations have either remained feudal or developed towards capitalism.

Internal Dynamics–External Factors

The first example with which I wish to develop the idea about the interaction between internal dynamics and external factors has to do with the civilizations of Central and South America which came into confrontation with Spanish and Portuguese colonialism. In the late fifteenth and early sixteenth centuries, these civilizations, *i.e.* the Aztecs, Incas, and Mayas, which lived in societies based on a communal order of production, came face to face with Spanish and Portuguese invaders who brought with them both firearms and contagious diseases. None of these native societies possessed the power to repel the physical repression coming from outside. They were defeated and exterminated en masse through the effects of firearms and disease. Another element which the raiders introduced was the horse, which was used as a major vehicle for waging war.[27]

Terrible genocides were perpetrated when waging war and peoples were completely wiped out. This gave rise to a great drop in production. No one was left to work in the fields or the mines, and this need for labor led to the enslavement of Africans.

Following this defeat, the dynamics of Central American and South American societies was altered according to the needs of Portuguese and Spanish colonialists. The economic structures, political relationships, social and cultural institutions, and religious beliefs were all organized to fit the needs of the colonialists. These societies could no longer live their own history but were forced to live that which was imposed upon them from outside. The same can be said for the native population of North America. Native-colonial interaction gave rise to a new synthesis, which then became a new thesis.

Even if the Aztec, Inca, Maya and other native American populations had been physically exterminated due to external factors, the above statement would hold true. But their culture, which cannot be extinguished through sheer physical might, still survives. For this reason, I believe that it is correct to say that the interaction between the internal dynamics of a colonized society and external factors leads that society towards a new synthesis. During this process, the raiding and occupying forces do not hesitate to annihilate those sectors of the native society which oppose them, as they try to consolidate a new social structure dependent on themselves, and one which acts as a bridge to the native society. Once they succeed in doing so, they stimulate the growth and development of this new structure through different means. From this point on, external powers determine the economic, political and social relationships in the colonized society.

The second example I would like to present is that of European imperialism and Africa in the eighteenth and nineteenth centuries. With the development of capitalism in Europe in the seventeenth and eighteenth centuries, two questions arose: (1) How to find and supply the metropolitan countries with raw materials; (2) How to find and expand new markets for manufactured goods. Such needs forced capitalist countries to spread outside of Europe and to plunder Africa.

Once colonial relations had been established, the question arose of how to keep the colonies constantly provided with administrators, missionaries, security forces, and other personnel. There also arose the issue of the enslavement of Africans and their exile to the Americas.

In those days African societies were chiefly based on hunting and gathering. Bows and arrows were in use. There was fishing and some horticulture. The Europeans came in with firearms and hunted down the African youth in their teens and twenties in the same way as animals were hunted. These youths were rounded up and sent to America to work on plantations, in mines, in construction, and in industry. Millions of Africans were transported to America in this way.

Nearly half of the youth being hunted in this inhuman, brutal way were killed in the course of being caught. A large portion of them died of torture, negligence, illness, hunger and thirst on the way. Those who did reach America were immediately forced into slavery. This human slaughter also led to a sudden break up in family and tribal relationships. The internal dynamics of traditional African societies were shattered by this imperialist and colonialist intervention. Although they tried with all their might to repel these invaders, their internal dynamics grew weaker. Gradually African societies became unable to live their own history and culture. Forced to devote much of their energy to security, they could not concentrate on production. In addition, there was the complication of native intertribal conflicts.

All these factors go to show how imperialist and colonialist actors managed to determine the development of entire nations. After shattering the internal dynamics of native African societies and forcing them to live a history imposed from the outside, Africa was finally formally divided and partitioned among European colonial powers in 1885. This division was carried out on the basis of who came first. With this criterion, different regions of Africa were bound to the economies of various metropolitan countries. To make this colonization appear legitimate politically, colonies with predetermined borders were established. It would be difficult to call these political units states, as their highest officials were Westerners appointed by the metropolitan country. The other administrators were all western-trained and educated natives who defended western interests. There was a collaborationist class who assisted the exploitation and plunder of the nation by the colonialists. Anyone who rebelled against the colonialists was immediately exterminated. Potential rebels were bought out through bribes and similar means. Opposition was scattered. Those who could not be bought out were annihilated. There was no question of the collaborationist class denying their own national identities, since, due to their dark skin, they were clearly not of British, French or any other European origin. Their religious beliefs were also different: they were animists. Due to their different skin colors and religious beliefs, there was no question of assimilating them. All possible measures were taken to ensure the spread of the collaborationist class.

The confluence of a society's internal dynamics and influences coming from without gives rise to a new synthesis. Due to the preponderant weight of the values being enforced from outside, however, this synthesis always safeguards the interests of the imperialist-colonialists. Africa is a good example to be studied in relation to the interaction of internal dynamics and external factors.

Our third case, Kurdistan, has to do with the carve-up of Kurdistan by the imperialists and their Middle Eastern collaborators in the 1920s. It was this process which has determined the ensuing course of development. The historical basis for the Kurdistan issue today lies in these events of the 1920s.

There have, of course, been other significant turning points throughout the course of Kurdish history. One of these was when the Kurds first encountered Islam and the Arab armies in the seventh century. Another was the appearance of the Oghuz Turks, who came from Central Asia via Iran to Kurdistan and Anatolia in the eleventh century. Later on, there were the Mongol invasions of the thirteenth century.

Situated in the center of the Middle East, the Kurds have not been able to live their own history, but have constantly confronted invading forces from outside. Their land is situated at a crossroads of civilizations which has been traversed by numerous invaders and occupying forces. Alexander the Great followed this path on his way east, as did the Persians on their way west. At later dates, the Romans, the Byzantines, and the Sassanids all made expeditions with the desire to dominate the region.

Furthermore the region was also manipulated by various states to settle scores with one another. Confrontations between the Sassanids and the Arabs, as well as between the Oghuz Turks and the Byzantines, were played out on Kurdish territory. The true goal of the Chaldiran Expeditions under Sultan Selim I (the Grim) in 1514 was to gain control of Kurdistan. The treaties between the Kurdish lords and the Ottoman regime in 1514 opened up an important period in Kurdish history.

All the wars and conflicts between the Ottoman and Persian empires took place in Kurdistan. This led to Kurdistan being divided in the first half of the seventeenth century. Later on, in the first part of the nineteenth century, the country was again divided when the northern part of Kurdistan on the Iranian side fell under Russian domination. The relations between the Kurds and Ottomans, as well as between the Kurds and Iran, throughout the nineteenth century are important chapters of Kurdish history worthy of further study.

The Significance of Divide and Rule

The tragedy of divide and rule politics became even clearer during the Iran-Iraq war. As is known, both Masoud Barzani, leader of the Kurdistan Democratic Party, and Jalal Talabani, leader of the Kurdistan Patriotic Union, were receiving support in their struggle against the Iraqi government from the Iranian regime throughout the war. At the same time, however, the same Iranian regime was engaged in full scale aggression against the Iranian Kurdistan Democratic Party under the leadership of Abdurrahman Ghassemlou which was waging its struggle within the borders of the Iranian state. Ghassemlou, in turn, was being supported by the Iraqi government. Under such conditions, how can these Kurdish leaders come together and develop joint policies for the struggle in Kurdistan? It is not possible. All they are doing is maintaining, even furthering, divide and rule politics. These policies reproduce themselves over and over.

With the escalation of PKK's activity inside Turkish borders, the same problem has surfaced. From time to time the various leaders in Southern Kurdistan have stated the following, "We have no conflicts with Turkey and desire to maintain friendship with the Turkish government. The PKK is Turkey's enemy. Turkey's enemy has no place on our soil. Whenever we see PKK, we will shoot them down. We will catch them and turn them over to the Turkish border authorities..." Whether or not the Kurdish organizations of Southern Kurdistan, especially the KDP, have actually done such things should be carefully looked into. But even the fact that

Turkish newspapers have printed such statements is a matter of no little significance in and of itself. There is no serious reason why there should be any hostility between the Kurdish organizations in the South and the PKK, while in contrast, there are many existing reasons for animosity between the former and the Turkish government, which has, among other things, carried out air and land raids in Southern Kurdistan under the pretext of "chasing away the brigands." Once again, all that is being done is the maintenance and furtherance of divide and rule policies.

The ample benefits provided to the *Jash* groups in Iraq, and the maintenance of the system of "village guards" in Turkey, are no more than continuations of divide and rule policies. Taking into consideration that some of these village guards in Hakkari, Siirt, and Van in the 1960s and 1970s were actually members of the Kurdistan Democratic Party, it becomes clear just how intensely and destructively such politics are being enforced.

Along with the use of force, financial incentives are also widely applied in this process. People whose patriotic sentiments who are weak are bought off and placed in the ranks of the anti-national liberation movement front. On a smaller scale, families and tribes are pitted against one another. These rivalries, which are known as blood feuds, can be characterized as another dimension of divide and rule. All of these factors make it apparent to what degree foreign factors determine economic and social development. The internal dynamics of a society are no longer capable of determining that society's historical course.

The collapse of feudalism and the rise of capitalism until its highest phase, imperialism, in Europe, was a process springing from the internal dynamics of European society. This same process, however, becomes one of external factors in relation to the backward colonialist societies when it comes to the spread of imperialism to all corners of the planet.

The consequences of Kurdistan's historical carving-up and loss of control over its own development are far graver today than they ever were in the past. The Kurdish nation at this time faces tremendous dangers, the first of which is chemical warfare. None of the states which colonizes Kurdistan has any difficulty in getting hold of chemical weapons. Even though they are aware of the significance of human rights, they have also realized that the key factor in determining international relations is trade. Given the lack of freedom of speech and freedom of the press in these countries, and the absence of popular control, or pressure groups capable of influencing the government and politicians, the administrations of these countries can go ahead and make use of chemical warfare against the

Kurds without paying any attention to grievances which may arise from international human rights organizations.

At the moment it is no longer possible for the national liberation struggle in Kurdistan to be brought to a halt through conventional methods of warfare. When it comes to chemical weapons, however, it is very difficult for the broad masses to protect themselves in any way; such weapons destroy not only people, but every living thing with which they come into contact. Not only is nothing left alive, but the land can no longer be used for agriculture. There is also another aim behind the use of chemical warfare, which is to drive the local population into exile, thus altering the demographic composition of the area.

Having been unsuccessful in their attempts to assimilate the Kurds through all sorts of racist policies, these colonialist states are now looking to the physical extermination of Kurds. The greatest factor at work in fortifying the nation's internal dynamics in the face of the destruction and repression coming from outside is the continued questioning and search for their own identities by the Kurds themselves. In essence, it is this questioning and search which has given rise to the massacres and genocidal policies against them. The colonialist state wants a target nation to be submissive to the fate being forced on it from outside. It is easy to rule a cowardly, obedient, and unresisting people. The tragedy of this fact has emerged with the struggle against the imperialist and colonialist forces. The latter are equipped with the latest weapons. They collaborate with each other in their efforts to obliterate the Kurds. As for the Kurds, divided, deprived of all national rights, lacking even colonial status, and sunk into a hell entirely surrounded by enemies, they wage their struggle for existence.

From what has been outlined above, it follows that the principle of the right of nations to self-determination is not correct simply because the Bolshevik leaders said so, or Lenin wrote about it, or because it was expressed by the American President Woodrow Wilson in his 14th Points. Life itself renders the existence and application of this principle mandatory. Having attained national consciousness, the Kurds are being subjected to genocidal policies by the states which colonize them. This brings up the Kurds' right to self-determination as an objective necessity. The states which jointly rule them have nothing to offer them but tyranny, massacre, and genocide. Given the fact that the Kurds' national consciousness is rising from one day to the next, putting this principle into practices emerges as an even greater obligation.

The Situation of Bureaucrats and State Employees

The society's loss of identity is reflected in other sectors as well. Along with the landlords, sheikhs, tribal chiefs, businessmen, and those working in the service sectors, this process can also be observed in the bureaucrats working for the state, both high-ranking officials and civil service employees.

So far I have been through four major police interrogations. Many of the police who arrested and interrogated me were of Kurdish origin, as were the torturers. It is not necessary for them to come out and say they are Kurds because it is made clear by their speech, attitudes, and behavior. These persons have identified with the official ideology in every sense of the word. They even propagated Turkism.

In June 1981, one of the policemen in the Ankara Police Headquarters shouted at me in rage:

"Now look here! There is no left or right! There is Ataturk! Come on. Write that down! Write down that everyone who lives in this country is a Turk!"

As he said this, the curses, insults, and torture carried on, on both his part and that of the other policemen in the room.

"I'm 27 years old. I'm a Kurd. I'm not mixed in these kinds of things. You're from Çorum. What do you need to mess with the Kurds for? Write down that everyone is a Turk!"

I replied, "You just said you were a Kurd. It wouldn't be very convincing for me to write down that everyone is a Turk."

The torturer went into an even greater rage. He was practically foaming at the mouth.

"What do you mean twisting my words around like that! Who do you think you are? Is that what you understood by what I said? Did I say such a thing?"

While in prison I observed that a large percentage of the guards were of Kurdish origin. There is certainly an element of tragedy in this. You want the Kurds to be able to lead a dignified life and possess rights on an equal basis with those of other nations. These "Kurds," however, blame you for your ideas and your efforts. They torture you. They stand in the front line when it comes to oppression, tyranny, and torture.

A number of reasons can be cited for the fact that most of the guards and prison officials are Kurds. The first of these is the widespread unemployment. The second and more important reason, however, is that people who grow up under colonialism tend to be cowardly and aggressive. They are not raised in a society which allows them to prove themselves. The only way to do so is to identify with the ruling nation, putting themselves in the role of the colonial administrations and behaving aggressively towards all those around them. The guards, especially those working in prisons, where political prisoners are kept, generally come from the lowest strata of society. In the prisons they find a scapegoat for the repression and backwardness they have themselves suffered—the political prisoners, on whom they vent all their rage and aggression. By fighting against communists and atheists, they seek to prove themselves.

The fact that most of the guards in the prisons where political prisoners are kept are of Kurdish descent has given rise to confusion amongst revolutionaries coming from the western part of Turkey. Whenever torture, tyranny, and prison are mentioned to them, these "Kurds" come to their minds. This is actually the natural result of the Kurds' subjection to so much inhumane, anachronistic treatment. Although most western revolutionaries are aware of this, the state is still hoping to benefit from this process.

Once again, when we take a closer look at police interrogations, we see that among the teachers/professors who act as informers, it is those of Kurdish origin who head the list. Such professors, who have totally identified with the official ideology, state that it is a crime for one to mention Kurds. They can be found on both the left and the right of the political spectrum. Governors, attorneys, and judges are no different. I encountered many such bureaucrats while conducting field trips in the 1960s. They defend the official ideology with fervor in both word and deed.

It should be kept in mind that for Kurds to have access to such posts is contingent upon denial of their ethnic identities. Although Kurds who identify with the official ideology and call themselves Turks are able to do just about anything, there are a still some fields from which they are generally excluded. The primary example is the fact that there are very few Kurds admitted to the Turkish military academy. As the national liberation movement gains ground, this number is becoming even fewer.

The number of bureaucrats of Kurdish origin is also minimal in institutions such as the Department of State Planning, the Bank of the Provinces, positions of decision making, and investment authorities.

In brief, we can say that Kurds in the state bureaucracy are in the same agent category as the Kurdish ruling classes. However, since a large percentage of them do not work in the Kurdistan region, they are not as obvious as the landlords, tribal chiefs, sheikhs and businessmen.

What about Kurdish musicians, writers, and dancers? Unlike their Turkish counterparts, whenever they make reference to their ethnicity, they are likely to be accused of being "nationalists," "racists," and "chauvinists." Is there not a contradiction between the fact that while any reference to Turkishness by a Turkish writer is considered natural, no Kurd can do the same thing without hesitation? Is it not sad that such Kurds, who hesitate to express their own true identities, are contributors to the enrichment of Turkish writing?

Can the same not be said for such professionals as doctors, lawyers, accountants, and engineers? In recent years there have been many indications that national consciousness is rapidly spreading amongst them, although it is still not enough to be called a strong current.

The Situation of Members of Parliament

It is of additional importance to consider and examine the situation of members of parliament within this framework and from the constitutional point of view.

The preamble of the Constitution of 1982 contains the following paragraphs:

> Following the operation carried out of 12 September 1980 by the Turkish Armed Forces in response to a call from the Turkish nation, of which they form an inseparable part, at a time when the approach of a separatist, destructive and bloody civil war unprecedented in the Republican era threatened the integrity of the eternal Turkish motherland and the existence of the sacred Turkish State,
>
> The Constitution was prepared by the Consultive Assembly, given final form by the Council of National Security, which are the legitimate representatives of the Turkish Nation, and adopted, approved and directly enacted by the Turkish Nation,
>
> And is entrusted for safekeeping by the Turkish Nation to the patriotism of its democracy-loving sons and daughters, so that it may be understood to embody the ideas, beliefs

and resolutions set forth below and be interpreted and implemented accordingly, commanding respect for, and absolute loyalty to its letter and spirit:

—The direction of concept of nationalism as outlined by Ataturk, the founder of the Republic of Turkey, its immortal leader and unrivalled hero; and in line with the reforms and principles introduced by him;

—The determination to safeguard the everlasting existence, prosperity and material and spiritual well-being of the Republic of Turkey, and to ensure that it attains the standards of Contemporary Civilization, as a full and honorable member of the world family of nations;

—Recognition of the absolute supremacy of the will of the nation, and the fact that sovereignty is vested fully and unconditionally in the Turkish Nation and that no individual or body empowered to exercise it on behalf of the nation shall deviate from democracy based on freedom, as set forth in the Constitution and the rule of law instituted according to its requirements;

—The understanding that separation of powers does not imply an order of precedence among the organs of the State, but reflects a civilized division of labor and mode of cooperation restricted to the exercise of specific State powers, and that supremacy is vested solely in the Constitution and the laws;

—The determination that no protection shall be afforded to thoughts and opinions contrary to Turkish national interests, the principle of the existence of Turkey as an indivisible entity with its state and territory, Turkish historical and moral values, or the nationalism, principles, reforms and modernism of Ataturk, and that as required by the principle of secularism, there shall be no interference whatsoever of sacred religious feelings in state affairs and politics;

—The understanding that it is the birthright of every Turkish citizen to lead an honorable life and develop his material and spiritual resources under the aegis of national culture, civilization and the rule of law, through the exercise of the fundamental rights and freedoms set forth in this Constitution, in conformity with the requirements of equality and social justice;

—The recognition that all Turkish citizens are united in national honor and pride, in national joy and grief, in their rights and their duties towards their existence as a nation, in blessings and in burdens, and in every manifestation of national life, and that they have the right to demand a peaceful life based on absolute respect for one another's rights and freedoms, mutual love and fellowship, and desire for, and belief in "Peace at home, peace in the world."

As is seen, the preamble of the Constitution contains such expressions as "The integrity of the eternal Turkish Nation and motherland," "The existence of the sacred Turkish State," "The fact that sovereignty is vested fully and unconditionally in the Turkish Nation," "Turkish National interests," "The principle of the existence of Turkey as an indivisible entity with is state and territory," "Democracy-loving sons and daughters of the Turkish Nation." In the Constitution of 1982, as well as that of 1961, it is stressed that the Constitution derives its speed and inspiration from Turkish Nationalism. The word "Turkish" is repeated 14 times in the preamble. Similar expressions exist in the articles of the Constitution.

In the section on "freedom of expression and dissemination of thought" (Article 26/3-4) it is stated that "No language prohibited by law shall be used in the expression and dissemination of thought. Any written or printed documents, phonograph records, magnetic or video tapes, and other means of expressions used in contravention of this provision shall be seized by a duly issued decision of a judge or, in cases where delay is deemed prejudicial, by the competent authority designated by law. The authority issuing the seizing order shall notify the competent judge of its decision within twenty-four hours. The judge shall decide on the matter within three days."

It is clear that this article of the Constitution prohibits the dissemination in languages other than Turkish, that is to say in Kurdish. This prohibition is peculiar to the Kurdish language since publications in English, French, German, Arabic, Armenian, Greek, Persian, and Hebrew languages are very easily made.

In the section on "Freedom of the Press" (Article 28/2) the restriction is made that "publications shall not be made in any language prohibited by the law."

In the section of "Rights and Duty of Training and Education" (Article 42/9) it is stated that "no language other than Turkish shall be taught as a mother tongue to Turkish citizens at any institution of training or education. Foreign languages to be taught in institutions of training and education and the rules to be followed by schools conducting training and education in a foreign language shall be determined by law. The provisions of international treaties are reserved."

Here it will be necessary to refer to the law which prohibits the Kurdish language. "The law concerning publications in languages other than Turkish." The first article of this law number 2932 and dated 19 October 1983, under the title of "Object and Content" states as follows:

> This law regulates the essentials and procedures about the prohibited languages in the expression and dissemination of thought, for the purpose of protecting the indivisible integrity of State with its territory and nation, sovereignty, national security and public order.

The second article under the title of "Languages Which Should not be Used in Expression and Dissemination of Thought" states:

> The expression, dissemination and publication of thoughts in any language other than the first official language of states which have been recognized by the Turkish state are prohibited. The provisions of international treaties which Turkey has taken part in, and laws and regulations relating to training, education, scientific research and publications of public institutions and establishments are reserved.

The third article identifies the mother tongue of Turkish citizens.

> The mother tongue of Turkish citizens is Turkish.
>
> a) All kinds of activities intending to use and disseminate languages other than Turkish as mother tongues are prohibited.
>
> b) In meetings and demonstration marches, without receiving permission from the highest local authority, even if not forbidden by this law, holding posters, placards, devices, framed inscriptions etc. and dissemination with phonograph

> records, magnetic or video tapes and other means and tools in a language other than Turkish are prohibited."

The 4th, 5th and 6th articles show penalties.

In accordance with the 134th article of the Constitution "The Ataturk High Institute of Culture, Language, and History" has been established. The article reads as follows:

> The Ataturk High Institute of Culture, Language and History shall be established as a public corporate body, under the moral aegis of Ataturk, under the supervision and with the support of the president of the Republic, attached to the office of the Prime Minister, and composed of the Ataturk Center of Research, the Turkish Language Society, the Turkish Historical Society and the Ataturk Cultural Center to conduct historic research, to produce publications and disseminate information on the thought, principles, and reforms of Ataturk, Turkish Culture, Turkish History and the Turkish Language.

These are some judgements of the Constitution which derive their inspiration from Turkish nationalism. In this connection, the 81st article on "Oath-taking" should also be pointed out. It reads as follows:

> Members of the Turkish Grand National Assembly, on assuming office, shall take the following oath:
>
> I swear upon my honor and integrity, before the great Turkish Nation, to safeguard the existence and independence of the State, the indivisible integrity of the Country and the Nation; the unconditional sovereignty of the Nation; to remain loyal to the supremacy of the law, to the democratic and secular Republic and to Ataturk's principles and reforms; not to deviate from the ideal according to which everyone is entitled to enjoy human rights and fundamental freedoms under peace and prosperity in society, national solidarity and justice, and loyalty to the Constitution."

On the other hand, there is an expression in the Constitution formulated as "the indivisible integrity of the State with its territory and people." This expression is repeated twice in the preamble of the Constitution and once in the 3rd article on the "Integrity of the State,

Official Language, Flag, National Anthem, and Capital," once in the 5th article on the "Fundamental Aims and Duties of the State," and once in the 13th article on "Restrictions of Fundamental Rights and Freedoms."

The slogan of "Indivisible integrity of the State with its territory and people" is repeated once in the 14th article on "Prohibition of Abuse of Fundamental Rights and Freedoms," three times in the 28th article on "Freedom of the Press," once in the 30th article on "Protection of Printing Facilities" once in the 33rd article on "Freedom of Association," once in the 58th article on "Protection of Youth" once in the 68th article on "Forming Parties, Membership and Withdrawal from Membership in a Party," and once in the 69th article on "Principles to be Observed by Political Parties."

It is also repeated once in all and each of the following articles: 81st article on "Oath-taking," 103rd article on "Oath-taking of the President of the Republic," 118th article on the "National Security Council," 122nd article on "Martial Law, Mobilization and State of War," 130th article on the "Institute of Higher Education," 133rd article on "Radio and Television Administration and News Agencies with State Connection," 135th article on "Public Professional Organizations," and 143rd article on the "Courts of the Security of State."

As seen, the expression of "The Indivisible Integrity of the State with its Territory and People" is repeated 22 times in separate parts of the Constitution. This is one of the most important points in the Constitution, which rejects and denies the national existence and ethnic identity of Kurds, and shows that one can benefit from various public liberties and social rights only by being a Turk, or becoming a Turk; in other words, by rejecting and denying Kurdish identity.

In the Constitution of 1961, this slogan is recorded only in the 3rd article. In this article on the "Integrity of the State, Official Language and Capital" it is stated that "The Turkish State is an indivisible whole with its territory and people."

In the Constitution of 1961, this is expressed as "Independence of the State, Integrity of Motherland and Nation" in the 77th article on "Oath-taking of Members of Parliament" and 96th article on "Oath-taking of the President of the Republic." Later on, during the regime of the 12 March 1971 Coup, the Constitution was subjected to very large amendments after which "The indivisibility of the State with its Territory and People" slogan was repeated in 13 different expressions. This slogan was added to some of the articles. The articles were rewritten in accordance with this slogans. For example, the heading of the 11th article was "The Essence of

Fundamental Rights" before the amendment; this became "The Nature of Fundamental Rights and Freedoms, Restriction and Prohibition of Abuse of Fundamental Rights and Freedoms." This slogan was repeated twice in this article but was repeated three times in the amended 22nd article on "Freedom of Press," once in the 26th article on "Right to Mass Media Other than the Press," twice in the 29th article on "Freedom of Association," once in the 46th article on "Right to Organize Labor Unions," once in the article on "Principles to be Observed by Political Parties." This form of expression is repeated once in the 121st article related to "Radio and Television Administration and News Agencies," and once in the 136th article related to "Organization of Courts."

Following military coups, either new constitutions are drawn up or existing constitutions are subjected to large amendments. In both cases keeping the Kurdish problem under wraps and taking new precautions is a basic concern. Any action is considered to deny the ethnic identity of Kurds and to reject their national rights. All measures thus taken are never questioned. These efforts betray one of the key reasons for military coups in Turkey.

As a conclusion I would like to point out that the Kurds in Turkey can be anything after denying their identity. They can be parliamentary members too. However, given these articles of the Turkish Constitution, is it credible to suppose that the Eastern members of the Turkish parliament who say they are Kurds are really Kurdish? Bearing these articles in mind, isn't parliamentary membership restricted by stipulations of denying Kurdishness, accepting Turkish identity, and contributing to Turkish propaganda?

What is the meaning of such official oath-taking?

The Kurdish Petty Bourgeoisie

We have already pointed out that it is up to revolutionaries and democrats to defend Kurdish national awareness. But who are these revolutionaries and democrats?

Students and religious men who have been educated in the medresses may fall into this category. These are elements capable of understanding the Kurdistan question within the context of Turkey, the Middle East, and the world, explaining the issue to their own people, and proposing solutions. They can comprehend Kurdistan's status as an international colony, and initiate discussion of the issue among a wider community.

For this very reason, imams educated at medresses were all removed from office following the coup of 12 March 1971. From that time on, all imams have been required to finish *İmam-Hatip* schools (secondary schools for the training of Islamic religious personnel). The main reason imams educated in the medresses, who are called mellas, possessed national awareness was due to the fact that education in these institutions was carried out in Kurdish. In addition to studying the Koran, there were also courses in Kurdish literature and history. There is certainly nothing of the sort in the İmam-Hatip schools.

The mellas are a typical Kurdish intelligentsia, which means they are aware of the problems of their own society and the ties between their own society and others. Only this intelligentsia can relate information, consciousness and new ideas to their own people and propose solutions. They are political persons, as differentiated from "intellectuals."[28]

As for students, the Ministry of Education does everything it can to keep them from gaining awareness of their own problems, especially the Kurdish national problem. Through the tireless repetition of the official ideology, enforcement of an educational system based on Ataturk, and never-ending repression and prohibitions, students are inundated with the concerns of Turkism and kept completely in the dark when it comes to the Kurdish community.

In spite of all these measures, the world is getting smaller and smaller. Mass communication is continually increasing in efficiency. The relationship between individuals and groups are becoming tighter. The spread of the national movement is leading to the questioning of the tribal structure and the traditional institutions. The students can no longer be isolated from this course of events.

Today, the younger generation of families who formerly took the side of the state in the repression of Kurdish uprisings are generally participants in the national liberation movement. On the other hand, youth coming from families who have conflicts with the state seem to be staying out of the movement. This phenomenon is worthy of further study.

The Kurdish petty bourgeoisie can be included in the category of revolutionaries and democrats. Craftsmen such as shoemakers, tailors, and carpenters, as well as professionals such as lawyers, doctors, and builders are all part of the movement. So are teachers, some office workers, barbers, painters and drivers. The landless peasants and those with very small parcels of land form an important base for the movement.

The position and attitudes of the Kurdish working class, such as in Batman and Tatvan, should be looked into. We do know which sectors of the workers play a significant role in the Kurdish movement.

The most important aspect of these relations, however, is the class basis for the various movements which have developed in Northern Kurdistan from the 1960s on. For example, the "49," who were arrested in late 1959,[29] or the "23," who were tried in 1963.[30] From what class, for instance, were the members of the Kurdistan Democratic Party founded in 1965? Who were the people who made up the "Eastern Group" of the Turkish Workers' Party which was formed in the 1960s? How did that party organize in the East?

What about the class composition of the persons who formed the Revolutionary Cultural Associations of the East in 1969? The class origins of the Kurdish members of the various Turkish and Kurdish left organizations should definitely be investigated.

Beyond all else, the PKK should definitely be studied carefully and thoroughly. How was this organization founded in the mid-seventies able to grow so quickly? Besides spreading geographically, the PKK has also been able to organize among social classes, something which no other Kurdish organization has managed to do. The trials of PKK members in the 1980s could be used as sources for gathering more information about the class basis of the PKK. Other factors, such as the age range of members, geographical origins of individuals, and especially the status of women in the organization, can provide invaluable information.

Colonial Intellectuals and Intellectuals of the Colonialist State: A Case Study

Tahsin Saraç died on 26 June 1989. Following his death, a number of articles were written about him by different writers and linguists in the press. All the articles praised his use of the Turkish language and his tremendous contribution to Turkish language and culture. His poems were said to have given a new depth for the Turkish language. Tahsin Saraç was a Kurd who denied his Kurdishness. He would say that his family came from Central Asia to Muş via Khorasan.[31]

Tahsin Saraç's life and work reflected the attitudes and behavior of colonial intellectuals. He put himself in the role of colonialists, since he knew that that was the road to intellectual circles and prestige in his colonialist society. This is how colonial intellectuals have been trained to think and act through their educational system. The same holds true for journalists and university professors. Besides, it is forbidden to be a Kurd anyway.

There is another thing which needs to be pointed out, however, in the case of Tahsin Saraç. He was very well travelled, and had frequent opportunity to meet up with different writers from different cultures all round the world. Many different languages and cultures were discussed at the meetings in which he participated. Sometimes the topic of repressed languages and cultures was brought up and resolutions were passed. The fact that Tahsin Saraç, after participation in so many such meetings, never remembered his own national identity really leads one to wonder... Tahsin Saraç and people like him are colonial intellectuals who do not accept being Kurdish. This is how they have earned the favor and esteem of the "intellectuals" of the colonialist state.

Singers

One of the more important policies flowing from the official state ideology has been the attempt to degenerate Kurdish music and culture. First, authentic Kurdish folk songs have been identified for degeneration. Special teams have been created, comprised of experts in folk music, literature, and dance, as well as military officers. Then the lyrics in the targeted Kurdish songs have been translated into Turkish and modifications made to the music. The melody has been altered in accordance with Turkish melodic patterns. The same piece has then been worked on by vocalists and specialists in folk music such as Mehmet Özbek. After all this, the piece has been performed on radio and TV, usually by vocalists of "Kurdish" origin. The latter have been preferred for two reasons—first, because their vocal chords are better adapted to the required sounds, and secondly, because the performance of these modified songs in Turkish by these vocalists gives a better return in the service of "Turkification."

We can characterize the contributions of these vocalists as the furtherance of cultural imperialism in Kurdistan. Moreover, this is also the usurpation of folk tradition. The song "White Rose, Red Rose" as sung by Mehmet Özbek, for example, which was chosen as Turkish Folk Song of the Year, is actually a Kurdish folk song. The same song, sung by Iraqi poet Tahsin Taha, was also made into a record in Iraq and can be heard frequently on Radio Baghdad. The title of the song in Kurdish is "Rabe Cotyar de Hilo Rabe." The authentic Kurdish version, however, is forbidden. Is this not a perfect instance of usurpation?

The popular song, "Let Me See You in the Garden," sung by Celal Güzelses, was also hailed as a Turkish folk song. In reality, this piece is a

Kurdish folk song sung on Radio Baghdad by the Cizre born vocalist Arif Jizravi. Its original title is "De Rabe Gula Bicinin."

An article which appeared in *Tempo* magazine on 9-15 April 1989, points out that although Kurdish is a forbidden language, there are actually many Kurdish songs being passed off as Turkish folk music on the market today.

Racist and colonialist writers such as Coşkun Kirca have written over and over that Kurdish is a primitive language, and that humanity, as well as the Kurds, would be better off were it to be wiped off the face of the earth. Let them try removing all the songs of Kurdish origin from TV and radio and we will see what is left.

Anyone who criticizes this usurpation of cultural tradition, however, finds himself in court under charges of "insulting the state." In spite of all the obstacles, however, we can be sure that in the near future we will witness an upsurge in the struggle for the defence of Kurdish culture.

Harold Pinter's play "The Language of the Mountains" is said to have been inspired by the playwright's observations of the situation of the Kurds in Turkey. In the play, a woman who does not speak the official language of the country, goes to visit her son in prison. The guards shout at the woman in an intimidating fashion, saying, "Your language no longer exists; it's forbidden, you can't speak the language of the mountains any more; you have to use the state language." The woman cannot speak with her son. In a second visit, she is told that the mountain language has been allowed until further orders are received, and she can speak to her son in that language. Her son tells her "Now we are free to speak our language," but despite all his pleading, she refuses to speak. She tries to express her rage and fury through her eyes and facial expressions. Silence and rage are one's first reaction to this situation and they can be considered the seeds of consciousness. The development of consciousness then leads to protest. The mother tries to express her protest through silence.

The Development of Capitalism in Kurdistan and the Kurdish National Movement

There is no doubt that the development of the Kurdish national movement is related to the development of capitalism in Kurdistan, although not in the way a theoretical model would lead us to believe. Theoretically, the ruling classes of an oppressed nation portray their own class interests as the interests of the entire nation to ensure their share of local markets. In Kurdistan, however, the landlords, sheikhs, tribal chiefs, and businessmen have all turned into agents, as we mentioned earlier. In addition to this, capitalism has also thrust the petty bourgeois and revolutionary elements into action. The increase in road networks, the influence of the mass media, the spread of education, and urbanization have brought the masses into close contact with each other, which has in turn accelerated the growth of the national movement.

Of course, the aim of the above-mentioned developments, such as the building of roads and communication systems was to further assimilation. Nevertheless, TV also brought news from the outside world, such as the struggles of the Palestinians, or the Turkish ethnic minority in Bulgaria. Such news items probably led to increasing questions and debates amongst the Kurds themselves. As for the roads, which were intended primarily for military use, they also allowed more frequent access to the cities. Dams, irrigation, and technological advances have raised the overall standard of living, increased the use of wage labor, and led to the dissolution of feudal ties. The spread of democracy has further accelerates this process.

The press coverage of two events in particular—the oppression of the Turkish ethnic minority in Bulgaria, and the Palestinian uprising, along with the predominant attitudes towards these events have been especially powerful in raising national consciousness amongst Kurds. Another event which has had a similar effect was the influx of Kurdish refugees from Iraq. The frequent reference to Iraqi Kurds by the media led to questions regarding why tribes and families had been broken up by false borders. Once such a process was underway, it could not be brought to a halt easily.

In the same way that capitalism alters the material structure of a fixed society and mobilizes the relations between man and the land, it also mobilizes people's mental structures. Numerous taboos are overcome, and certain facts which have been concealed for long periods are brought out into the open. This leads to an unmasking of the system itself, with all its weaknesses in plain sight for everyone to see.

With the initiation of substructural investments for the development of capitalism in Kurdistan in the 1950s, it was thought that possible "nationalist" developments could be prevented through the enforcement of assimilation. This policy seemed to have succeeded in the fifties. By the late sixties, however, things began to change. The establishment of the Revolutionary Cultural Associations of the East in 1969 brought assimilation to a halt. Social and political opposition had begun. As for today, there is no longer any hope for assimilation to succeed. Even those who know Turkish well insist on defending themselves in the courts in their native tongues, Kurdish, in spite of the harsh consequences.

Historical and social consciousness are spreading fast. Just as capitalism cannot be stopped, these developments cannot be halted either. All of this is actually tightly linked to the issue of progress in the "East."

Some Comments on Progress in the "East"

The Kurdish question is referred to by the state, universities, political parties, etc., as the Eastern Question. They explain it by saying that due to geographical reasons, the presence of feudal institutions in the East, and widespread ignorance, the East is a backward region. According to the official view, there is nothing more to the issue than the need to overcome this economic backwardness.

It is worth our while to take a closer look at some of the solutions proposed for progress in the region. The first of these, known as state incentives, advocates the view that progress in the East cannot be achieved through private initiative. The Republican Peoples' Party and the political institutions which spring from this tradition support this point of view. To a certain degree, it is also advocated by other political parties. In other words, they say that not much has been done in the East, but promise to provide certain things for the people there.

The chief error in this proposal is that it is difficult to maintain a predominantly state run economy in the East, while capitalist development is overriding throughout the rest of Turkey. On the other hand, state planning regarding the East is primarily orientated towards military objectives. For the state, the main problem is to get rid of the Kurdish issue altogether. In fact, the state actually denies the existence of the problem. Whenever the issue of investments to develop water systems, road networks, electricity, dams, factories, or telephones is brought up, they calculate what contribution such investments will have on the ultimate goal of assimilation. When they build roads, for instance, they do so that tanks, soldiers, and weapons may be brought into the area. When they build schools they calculate whether or not these schools will be suitable for use as police stations and prisons. It is dubious whether or not these investments in the name of progress will actually overcome the economic backwardness of the area.

Moreover, bribes, corruption and favoritism are rampant in state enterprises. Such enterprises are usually poorly run and nonproductive.

The second road proposed for bringing about progress in the East is that of private enterprise. This view has become increasingly popular since Turgut Özal became Prime Minister. Numerous incentives have been provided to get Westerners to invest in the East. Brick and cement factories, cotton mills, dairy and breeding farms are given ample credit, as is the food processing industry and export oriented production. Substructural investments such as road-building, water, electricity and sewage systems are contracted out to Western firms.

In addition to ample credit, there are also other incentives such as duty-free machinery, tax reductions and the like, which are intended to encourage Western investors to invest in the East. The same incentives are not provided for investment in the West. Nevertheless, Western industrialists are still balking at investing in the East. This was quite obvious in the eighties. Western industrialists regard investing in the East as too risky due to the existence of the Kurdish question. Thus, they are of no help in bringing about economic progress in the East.[32]

In my opinion, the only force capable of actually bringing on progress in the East is a nationally aware Kurdish bourgeoisie. As we mentioned earlier, the state does everything in its power to prevent Eastern businessmen from investing in the area. Kurdish industrialists will only emerge as a strong and permanent force following a period of resistance and struggle. The crucial factor is consciousness, but as we have already mentioned, the younger generation of the Kurdish ruling classes have begun to break away from the agent characteristics of their fathers and forefathers. The seeds of such a bourgeoisie with national consciousness began to take root in the eighties.

Of course, socialists also have ideas and plans for the economic development of Kurdistan. These are dealt within the programs of the various socialist parties. Here we have tried to touch on some aspects of what has been done in the past within the framework of the events of today.

Lately, the Turkish government and to a certain extent the Turkish press, have been announcing increases in investments in the East, greater budget allocations, and the tremendous expenses the state is incurring for progress in the East. When we take a closer look, however, we see that such expenditures have been overwhelmingly used for police stations, prisons, roads for military use, housing for police and military personnel, development of communication networks, etc. Both the number of military posts and the number of officials on duty have increased considerably. Certain districts have more than a hundred military posts! While each of the stations formerly had some eight or nine soldiers on duty, they now have sixty or seventy. Some fifty new prisons have been constructed in the last few years and more are on the way.

The number of village guards has been increased to raise the efficiency of Kurd against Kurds operations. The salaries paid to these guards are constantly being raised so as to attract more people to the job. In addition, efforts are being made to increase the numbers of special forces units and informers. All of this takes money. This, then, is what is meant by the increase in budget allocations for the East!

GAP, which has also required tremendous government expenditures, is obviously a project intended mainly for the benefit of Western Turkey. It should not be forgotten that Kurdistan possesses huge amounts of natural resources such as petroleum, coal, phosphate, chrome, copper, iron, and water. One would expect countries colonizing Kurdistan to make such investments.

The Material Basis for the Weaknesses in Kurdish Society

A) The writings of Ehmede Xani, P. Auryanot, and Cigerxwin

Prior to determining the material causes behind Kurdistan's subjection to a policy of divide and rule, there are three works which, although they may appear to contradict one another, actually complement each other and help our comprehension of various processes at play.

The first of these is the work *Mem-u Zin* by Ehmede Xani, which contains an exuberant sense of national awareness. The Kurds and Kurdish language are referred to in Chapters Five and Six. With profound national feelings, one could even say national consciousness, it is explained why Kurds are a condemned people. Ehmede Xani is deeply troubled over the division of the Kurds between the Ottoman and Persian empires. Half the Kurds are engaged in fighting for the Ottomans and the other half for the Persians, while nothing is being done to strengthen their own society and leave an inheritance for future generations. Their lack of inter-Kurdish alliances leads to no good end. Here, Ehmede Xani is reproachful of Kurds and makes it known that he writes in Kurdish so that no-one can accuse Kurds of being without knowledge and substance. He respectfully pays tribute to the Kurdish poets of past centuries such as Harirli Ali (eleventh century), Sheikh Ahmed Mala-i Zivri (twelfth century), and Feki Teyran (14th century). Ehmede Xani's Arabic-Kurdish dictionary, written in 1648, was intended for use by Kurdish children.

In the original Kurdish version of the above mentioned work, *Mem-u Zin*, although not found in the Turkish translation, are twelve couplets which address the negative conditions under which Kurds are forced to live.[33]

After reading the work, one is forced to wonder why the society which gave birth to seventeenth century poets who were able to express their national feelings with such purity and exuberance has not been able to pull itself together. Why was such a society continually subject to divisions and exploitation by others? Why has a political consciousness not arisen amongst them?[34]

The second book I would like to mention was written by a Russian military officer. He also mentions the weakness of Kurdish national feeling in a book entitled *Russia, Turkey, the Persian Wars, and Reflections in the Situation of the Kurds in Turkey-Iran-Russia in the Nineteenth Century*. The book was published by the Caucasian Bureau of the Hamidiye Cavalry in 1899.

The book contains a number of noteworthy observations. He states that in the 1870s his troops assaulted a tribe of Kurds along the banks of the River Arax, resulting in a violent battle. Kurds belonging to other tribes stood by and watched without making the slightest attempt to aid their fellow Kurds against the Russian invaders. They even assisted the latter in achieving an easier victory. In fact, the Russians were also making preparations to settle accounts with those Kurds as well within a week's time. In addition to pointing out the weakness of a national awareness among the Kurds, Auryanot also refers to Kurds as savages, brigands and blunderers.

I think there must be an element of truth in P. Auryanot's observations on the national feelings of Kurds. The ease and extent with which the *Jash* in Iraq and the village guards in Turkey were organized can be taken as another example of a lack of Kurdish national awareness.[35] It is worth reflecting on the possible material basis for such attitudes and behavior. The herder economy and the tribal structure are two important clues.

The third work I would like to address belongs to Cigerxwin, a great Kurdish poet of the twentieth century, who lived in all parts of Kurdistan. His work *Shehr-i Jin* (The City of Life) differs from the two previously mentioned works in that in also proposes a solution.

The plot of *Shehr-i Jin* is as follows:

There is a young man named Hoyrat, who is constantly on horseback, riding from one mountain to the next, showing off, and doing all sorts of tricks to draw attention to himself. He feels no responsibility to anyone in life. He just lives from day to day, constantly moving on and on. One day, after some adventure in the mountains, he comes across a withered old woman in distress. The woman is a captive in enemy hands; her hands and feet are bound by chains. She is suffering great torment and surrounded by numerous enemies. The young man feels much sorrow on seeing the woman in this condition and wants to approach her directly to find out who she is and how she ended up in this dreadful condition.

As the youth draws nearer to the woman, she begins to appear younger and more beautiful. A happiness dawns inside him. Those who are holding the woman captive, however, prevent him from approaching her. In the meantime, the woman's body begins to writhe with spasms. Sores and cracks appear on some of her limbs. Her captors begin to rough her up, which makes her grow old and ugly again.

The young man refuses to give up in his search to find out who the woman is and how she fell into such a situation Despite all the guards and endless precautions, he approaches her secretly and finds out who she is.

He finds out that the woman is his mother, and is immediately struck by the thought that, although he must have a mother, he had never thought about her. He is overwhelmed by the realization that up until then he had been completely indifferent. He wonders why it had never occurred to him to find out who his mother was, or whether he had any brothers and sisters. The more he thinks, the more he realizes what difficulties he is up against.

The youth makes up his mind to rescue the old and distraught woman bound in chains. From then on, he no longer uses his talents for showing off. He no longer wields the sword for others. He uses all his abilities to rescue his mother. He constantly searches for and finds ways to hold meetings with her, in the course of which, he finds that he has other brothers as well.

The young man's brothers are called Agha, Shih, Ashir, Bajari, Hakim and Renchber. He goes out to look for them, and finds them one by one, with the exception of Renchber, telling each of the wretched situation of their mother and why they must rescue her. None of the brothers know that they had a mother and lived for themselves alone. They are rich, happy and free from anxiety. They cooperate with their captors as loyal assistants. They refuse to accept the young man as their brother. They did not even known they had such a brother. They had not even been aware that they were brothers themselves. They were always quarrelling and blaming each other.

The young man is greatly troubled by the callousness and irresponsibility of his brothers. He discovers that he will not receive any assistance from them in rescuing their mother. Finally he goes in search of his last brother Renchber, who turns out to be a poor man who spends all his time in the fields struggling along with a primitive plough and has no expectations whatsoever from life. He is also a foolish fellow with a head as thick as stone through which nothing could pass.

The young man, however, is determined to rescue his mother. Despite all the obstacles, he feels that only Renchber can be of assistance to him. He never breaks off his relations with Renchber. Eventually he sees that Renchber is not at all as foolish as he appears. He has just been offended and is angry. He knows about his mother and brothers, and one by one explains how it is they who impoverished him. He then cites all the injustices to which he has been subjected. They decide to rescue their mother but are only able to do so after fighting not only against their enemies, but also against those who were responsible for allowing their mother's to end in such a wretched state.

Although *Sheh-i Jin* is briefly summarized here, it is actually a very long legend with revolutionary undertones, where rebellion is represented as a positive process. In my opinion, Cigerxwin had a very clear perception of the class situation in Kurdistan. There are certainly material reasons why the landlords, tribal chiefs, and bureaucrats turned their backs on their own kin. It is necessary to probe these reasons.

B) Herding and the Characteristics of the Tribal Structure

Kurdistan is a generally mountainous area whose inhabitants are primarily occupied with raising livestock, an occupation which requires extensive pastures. These pastures are used by families and tribes who never allow others to enter or make use of their particular territory. This is because without extensive landholding it is not possible to increase the size or one's number of herds. For anyone else to make use of existing pastures, that would mean the reduction of their own grazing land. Under these conditions Kurds remained isolated from one another while individual tribes developed into closed structures which kept a distance from one another. Consequently, everyone was busy struggling to keep other tribes away from their own pasture land. This led to the development of armed forces, to which the hierarchic tribal structure was already predisposed. However, as the number of herds increased, there was also the need to increase one's grazing territory, which meant going to war with one's neighbors. Organizing raids on neighboring tribes was an important aspect of tribal relations.

The preoccupation with finding pastures must have been a major factor in preventing intertribal unity. This same problem exists where there are societies whose primary livelihood is raising livestock. Agriculture, on the other hand, is a more labor-intensive activity. Families develop friendly and neighborly relations while toiling in the fields. Communication is widespread. This is certainly an environment more suitable to the development of national feelings. While families engaged in herding tend to close ranks against all outsiders, agriculture leads to the formation of a broad social network.

Clearly, within such a framework, people will tend to think only of themselves and their families. The compromises made with various invaders from outside were done so on the basic condition of no interference in the tribe's internal affairs. If the tribe was not able to safeguard its internal order from invaders or raiders, it became the slave of other raiding tribes and lost its own identity.

C) Kurdistan's Position at the Crossroads of Invasions and Migrations

Within such a "free" life-style, whenever there is a threat of invasion, rather than banding together with other tribes of the area to defend the region, each tribe seeks to fend for itself. As long as it is able to safeguard its own grazing land, it may find ways to compromise by cooperating with the invading forces. Such alliances can only work against other tribes. Each tribe renders its own existence subject to the invading force with which it has entered into alliance. In this way it maintains its own "free" life-style rather than being enslaved. At the same time, however, it is unable to come together with other tribes and to form a strong central power against invaders; thus they are unable to defeat invaders collectively.

This means that raising livestock and the institution of raiding have to be looked at within the same context. In certain places there are tribes which raise livestock and possess previously determined summer and winter pastures. Everyone defends their own pastures against everyone else. This was the economic and social order of the Kurds at the time of the Arab invasions, or the spread of Islam, in the seventh century. In my opinion, the Kurds did not try to fight off the invaders by forming alliances amongst themselves; instead, each tried to defend their own pastures. This led them to cooperate with the invaders on an individual basis, which in turn inflicted damage on neighboring tribes. Gradually, Kurds became a people who proved their existence through fighting in the service of others rather than themselves.

There are others, however, who do not agree with this explanation and say that it is not true that the Kurds did not fight against the Arab-Islamic invasions as one united force. According to those who espouse this view, the Arab-Islamic invaders encountered a Kurdish army of that day, fought bloody battles with them, and emerged victorious. Elderly Kurds who were captured were killed on the spot, while young men and women were sold off as slaves and concubines in the markets in Medina.

Similar events took place during the invasion of the Oghuz Turks from Central Asia in the eleventh century. At that time the invasions served to further deepen existing conflicts between Kurdish tribes. Works on Kurdish history, rather that pointing out the difference between the Kurds and other nations, are always trying to link them to either the Arabs, Persians, or Turanians, depending on whatever state the writers happen to come from. Without a doubt, these interpretations of history are little more than fairy tales, although they are important in that they are an indication of other people's attitude towards Kurds.

In addition to the above, the fact that Kurdistan was located along travel routes from East to West and West to East prevented the stabilization of any centralization that may have sprouted. Furthermore, not only did all the Ottoman-Persian wars take place on Kurdish territory, but both sides fought with armies heavily comprised of Kurdish recruits. The two empires repeatedly made use of Kurdistan as a buffer zone.

In addition to being herders, the Kurds were also nomads. The fact that some tribes took to the mountains to avoid fighting invaders, while others found ways to compromise, reduced any centralization tendencies among the tribes. However, I am not pretending to interpret Kurdish history going back thousands of years. This is not my field—but I am trying to develop several hypotheses concerning the material basis for the division of Kurdistan.

Another question which needs to be solved is the reason Kurds accepted Islam and not Christianity, and why they did not fight to maintain their own religion, Zoroastrianism. I think Kurds probably adopted Islam without entering into long wars. Islam was imposed as the religion of the state. Isolated tribes could not have been able to offer much resistance to the powerful Islamic invaders. Only by going along with the invaders, or obeying them, were they able to maintain their existence and life-style. At the same time, the invaders exploited the tribes for their own ends, especially as warriors, who were mostly employed to fight against other tribes. Christianity in contrast, developed as a religion of the downtrodden, the religion of those rebelling against the state. Thus, originally, it was not enforced through invasions. I believe that there are great differences between Christianity and Islam regarding the conditions under which they first emerged and developed.[36]

Another interpretation of the history of the Kurds in the pre-Islamic period is that long before the appearance of Islam they had ceased to live as herder-nomads and had begun settling and working the land in Mesopotamia. Various civilizations arose from these communities, which existed side by side with the Arabs. Following the introduction of Islam and up to the Emevi period, however, the Arab tribes, with the support of the state, waged a merciless war against the Kurds, who were forced to take to the mountains to seek protection. Thus, a life-style based on herding, tribal relations, and nomadism was reintroduced. This point of view is also shared by Ziya Gokalp.[37]

On the other hand, some sources state that a large number of Kurds did adopt Christianity, but after the majority had become Muslim, most of them became Muslim as well. Kurds who remained Christians began living with Armenians. These Christian Kurds live primarily in the region of Yerevan today.

Centralization tendencies among the Kurds became stronger in the tenth and eleventh centuries at the time of the weakening of the Abbasid Empire. These tendencies were especially pronounced in the regions of Greater Lor and Lesser Lor in Eastern Kurdistan, and amongst the Mervanis, who lived in the region of Diyarbekir and Cizre, as well as the Hansanveyhi of Southern Kurdistan. The state of Saladin, which flourished during the same period, was also founded by a Kurdish dynasty. With the influx of the Oghuz from Central Asia, however, these centralization tendencies were brought to a halt. The Kurds were unable to establish stable political structures. They continued to live as isolated tribes. With the later Mongol invasions, this instability and lack of centralization were further reinforced.

D) The Natural Resources of Kurdistan

By the late nineteenth century the West had discovered the great wealth in natural resources in Kurdistan and western powers began to compete with each other for it. Gradually, these raw materials became a great detriment to the Kurds. Once the imperialist powers understood that none of them would succeed in gaining possession of Kurdistan in its entirety, they decided that the best thing to do would be to divide and share it. Thus, in addition to tribal social structures as herders, and their location on so many invasion and migration routes, the natural resources of Kurdistan also emerged as factors working against Kurds. All of these facilitated Kurdish disunity and the partition of Kurdistan amongst foreign powers.

Natural resources may be a great source of prosperity for a nation. For the Kurds, though, who were unable to achieve self-determination, such resources resulted in the opposite. All the struggles waged by the Kurds for self-determination were drowned in blood by the intervention of imperialist and colonialist states.

E) Kurdish Tribes as a Political Structure

Kurds are not the only society to be organized on a tribal basis. The Turks and Mongols in Central Asia, as well as the Arabs in the Middle East, and the Berbers in North Africa were all tribal societies as well. The tribe is a nomadic group claiming blood ties and descent from a common ancestor, and possessing a common language and tradition. The tribe (*ashiret*) is the largest unit of the three units composing Kurdish society. The smallest is the family, with the sub-tribe (*kabile*) in between. Both of the two larger structures are based on lineage and descent. Lineage (*soy*) amongst the Kurds, as with other tribal societies, is reckoned by tracing one's ancestry back to a common ancestor. To be able to trace one's ancestry further back than others is considered a matter of great honor. From this emerged the tradition of boasting of one's ancestry, which is one of the key traditions of Kurdish society. Although most tribes (*ashirets*) are herder-nomads, those who have settled on the land still preserve this tradition. Nevertheless, settlement necessitates agricultural activity. In time, persons from outside the tribe are taken in, especially captured women and slaves. Following intertribal wars, members of weak and disintegrating tribes are added to those of victors as *rayas* or subjects.

The sub-tribe (*kabile*) emerged as a necessity for production and has an economic basis. It emerged from the need for power in herding and agriculture in competition against hostile tribes during summer and winter migrations, and when facing natural calamities. Exogamy, or marriage outside the sub-tribe, is the rule, although endogamy may occur as well if required. Within the sub-tribe, lineage in reckoned through the paternal side. Name, honor, and inheritance are reckoned according to paternal descent.

The means of production within the sub-tribe are communally owned. A leader is elected from the tribal elders. Decisions are made by the entirety of the adult men and women who come together as a body. Disintegration of the sub-tribe began with the division of labor and the emergence and spread of private property.

The Kurdish family is defined on the basis of the extended rather than nuclear family. The family generally consists of a grandfather, his sons, and their families. The sub-tribe (*kabile*) consists of a number of such families, while the tribe (*ashiret*) may consist of anywhere from three to ten sub-tribes. The number of sub-tribes may increase with population growth, acquisition of pasture lands, and the addition of outside elements. This leads to the expansion of the tribe, a process which is at the expense of other tribes. The name, honor, and prestige of the tribe is reckoned on the basis of how far back the lineage can be traced.

The tribe can also be looked upon as an administrative and political unit. It is like a state on a miniature scale, with a hierarchy extending all the way from the chief down to each tent. Due to the fact that it is based on blood ties, as well as being an institution where orders are the rule, the tribe is an institution based on strict discipline. This discipline, however, reigns only in internal affairs; external relations between tribes are characterized by anarchy. Whenever a tribe catches local people or other tribes off guard, it tends to attack and plunder them. Every possible measure is taken to plunder the surplus production of settled communities.

One step beyond the tribe is the tribal confederation. For this to be formed, a number of tribal chiefs have to turn over certain powers to a single leader, and this very rarely comes about. Rivalry over name, honor, and lineage is an obstacle to its realization. Thus, it only becomes possible when one tribe is so powerful that it is able to extract taxes from the others. This is an important stage in the formation of a central state.

Why Was There No Kurdish State in the Middle East? Why was Divide and Rule Imposed on the Kurds?

The absence of surplus production under the tribal system led to continual attacks and plunder of other tribes, which meant that there was constant fighting. The *Sherefname*, from beginning to end, deals with this anarchy. The economic basis for this warfare was because surplus production was barely enough to cover tribal needs, which meant that the goods of others were constantly sought after.

The fact that there is no such concept as the expropriation of unearned income in tribes is due primarily to the existence of blood ties between all tribal members, and this absence prevents the development of struggles against tribal chiefs. This was not the situation during the time of feudalism in Western Europe. There, the serfs worked the land of the lord, who expropriated the surplus produced by the former. Thus, confrontations could and did arise.

In tribal sources, such as that of the Mongols and Turks prior to settlement, the concept of property ownership was very weak. Where respect for property has not yet developmed, the concept of justice tends to be little known as well. One invaded and occupied other societies whenever and wherever one had adequate military strength to do so. The invaders then declared everything belonging to the invaded people to be their own, and the rights of the latter were rendered invalid.

There is also an opposing view that states that the concept of unearned income, or the expropriation of the surplus of others, actually does exist in tribal societies. This leads to the developed of private property and thus to struggles. Such situations emerge upon the permanent settlement of tribes and the beginning of agriculture. Nevertheless, the claims made in one's name, lineage, and honor still continue following such settlement. This is one of the major weaknesses of Kurdish society. Where so many tribes are preoccupied with competing with one another over name, lineage and honor, it is extremely difficult to reach statehood. A state can only arise with the presence of a centralized authority which has gained considerable strength over a wide territorial expanse. Kurdistan's rough, mountainous terrain was also an obstacle to such a process. High mountains, deep valleys, wide rivers, and the lack of a sufficient communications network were all factors which encouraged the continuation of autonomous local structures in the place of a centralized authority.

In the words of Ibn Khaldun, "In a land where there are many tribes and a variety of religious communities, the establishment of a strong and stable state is highly improbable."[38]

In a place such as Kurdistan, where so many tribes lived alongside one another, it is not unusual that Kurds never submitted themselves to a higher authority. Some Kurds also remained outside the tribal system. These groups lived in communities located in remote and precipitous places and had little or no contact with the armies of the Arabs, Seljuks, Turks, and Mongols. In many cases, Armenians and Assyrians, and later on Turks, Circassians, and others lived in close proximity to Kurds. Muslims, Christians, Jews and Zoroastrians could all be found living on Kurdish territory. The Kurds themselves are divided into Alevi, Sunni, Yezidi, Shafli and Hanefi.

One major aspect of tribal life is that work is not encouraged. This is a system based on social ranking. It is considered shameful for those belonging to the tribe to do work such as cutting and carrying wood. Such chores are to be performed by the *rayas*, while the members of the tribe perform such functions as hunting and fighting in wars. This is another reason why Kurdish social structure remained stagnant instead of being open to the introduction of capitalism.

Of course, tribal structures are not exclusively Kurdish. They can also be found in all nomadic societies. In fact, the tribal structure was of great benefit to the British in breaking up Arab society into numerous states in the early twentieth century. The Arab tribes have always been adamant in their refusal to submit to one another, which meant that it was quite easy to create a number of different states in place of one large centralized one.

What Is Meant By The Phrase "The Kurds Are Too Fond of Their Freedom"?

It is often stated that Kurds are excessively fond of living freely and independently, and that they never submit to other authorities. If this phrase refers to their relations amongst themselves, it can be said to apply on an individual basis. What happens, however, when it comes to safeguarding this freedom and national honor against the oppression and tyranny of those who rule them? Are they even able to preserve the desire for freedom against these states?

Countless events have taken place which belie and prove the falseness of the above cliches. Let's take a look at what happens in the case of blood feuds, for example. Everyone knows how manly(!), brave(!), and heroic(!) the Kurds are at such times. They can kill each other without flinching. They kill and wound each other as if it were nothing, even though it is usually their own relatives from the same or neighboring tribes. All this is done in the name of "defending their honor" and "not allowing others to trample on their dignity."

At a certain point, however, as the two opponents begin to tire, the gendarmes intervene. Then, those same people who had been doing everything within their might to kill each other, who had been roaring at each other like fearless lions, are suddenly transformed into sad and pitiful spectacles. Without the slightest difficulty, the gendarmes clap on the handcuffs and scuttle the lot of them off to headquarters. Even a sergeant or a rank and file soldier is able to do this. They beg and plead and try to make the authorities feel sorry for them. Usually their wives and children are bound and handcuffed and hauled off to jail along with them.

At the jail the women, especially the young women, are locked up in separate places where the police try to rape them. These manly(!) fellows who initiated the blood feud to safeguard their "honor" and "self-respect" know exactly what goes on, but do not dare to utter a murmur of protest.

What kind of freedom is this, I would like to ask? Is this what happens when people are too fond of their freedom, independence, honor and self-respect?

Of course, there is a reason behind such behavior, which we will go into.

What I am trying to point out here is that there is a difference between freedom on an individual basis and freedom on a national basis. They contradict each other. As we said, the herder life-style and isolation from one another prevented the development of national awareness. One's only loyalty were to the tribe, and loyalty to chiefs meant the presence of impenetrable walls between tribes. Only with the destruction of these walls could national awareness grow, but only with the growth of national awareness could such walls be destroyed so that loyalty to the nation could supersede loyalty to the tribe.

Clearly, individuals raised in such an environment tend to be selfish and preoccupied only with their own personal freedom, which can be accomplished through finding ways to accommodate outside intervention. Throughout history, the Kurds always preferred this way of doing things, making deals with the invaders. They were unable to secure a mechanism capable of driving away the invaders and defending the nation as a whole. They were submissive as long as they were allowed to manage their own internal affairs themselves. In this way the whole nation was gradually enslaved for the sake of individual freedom. Through the policy of "every tribe for itself" they became perfect targets for the implementation of divide and rule by the invaders. The Kurds today are an enslaved society. With a population of over 30 million, they are an enslaved people lacking even the status of a colony.

Individual freedoms and national enslavement are nothing more than two faces of the same coin. Only through sacrificing certain individual freedoms for the sake of national freedom can the latter be achieved. Up until now, Kurds have never known how to die for the sake of national freedom and independence. They have been too busy wiping out each other in blood feuds, many of which were actually provoked by the state. Of course there are no real individual freedoms without the existence of national freedom. What matters is not knowing how to die in a blood feud, but knowing how to die to deliver one's nation from slavery.

In this respect the emergence of the PKK is a turning point in the history of Northern Kurdistan. The PKK has taught us that one needs to be willing to die to achieve national liberation. It is just this consciousness, awareness, and determination which has thrown the fascist and colonialist Turkish state into a fever of anxiety.

In general, the Social Democrats and Marxist left in Turkey do not formulate their politics according to the will of the Kurdish people. This is understandable. What is not understandable, however, is why the Kurds try to formulate their politics in accordance with the Turkish left and Turkish Social-Democrats. If the Kurds believe they have certain rights, it should not make any difference to them what others have to say on the subject. If they feel that they have a natural right to speak and write Kurdish, they should do so without waiting for the laws to be changed. What good does it do to try and convince certain prominent Turkish racists and colonialists such as Prof. Mümtaz Soysal, Uğur Mumcu, and İsmail Cem that they deserve this most natural right? They should just go ahead and do it, and then, if they find themselves facing legal proceedings they can throw all their energy into developing a thorough defence of their actions.

Village Guards: An Indication of the Weakness of Kurdish Society

Following the commencement of guerrilla warfare in Turkey in August 1984, the system of village guards was developed as a means to contain and combat the guerilla movement. The security of the villages was to be ensured by these guards, who were selected amongst local peoples and provided with arms by the state. Most of the time the villagers selected were forced to accept the position. Such guards were offered generous salaries as well as premiums on the head of each dead guerrilla they brought in, the amount depending on the guerrilla's rank, to make such positions attractive.

Beyond all this, however, to increase the number of guards, the state negotiated with common criminals, especially murderers, by offering to release them from prison if they agreed to do this kind of work. Criminals who had escaped from prison were told that their cases would be closed and that they would no longer be sought after. Since 1985, a great deal of heavy bargaining has gone on between high state officials and tribal chiefs on this account, and many guards have been recruited in this way. Of course, since such deals are against the law, there is no written documentation, but it is commonly known that this takes place. A typical example is the case of the Jirki tribe in Beytulşebap. In 1975, during a circumcision ceremony for the son of the tribal chief, Tahir Adiyaman, a fight broke out between the provincial governor (*kaymakam*) and the district prosecutor. The kaymakam slapped Tahir Adiyaman in front of all the members of the tribe, which led to a shoot-out resulting in the killing of six gendarmes. The kaymakam and the district prosecutor ran away to save their own lives, and the tribe took to the mountains, where they remained for ten years. They finally came down in 1985 in response to the offer of pardon for those who agreed to work as guards.[39]

These guards are a major apparatus of terror. In some regions the gendarmes and soldiers turn people they have caught over to the guards, who torture them in the cruellest ways, cutting off their ears and noses, gouging out their eyes, or hacking them into pieces. The primary function of the guards, however, is to intimidate and terrorize the people amongst whom the guerrillas live and work, rather than deal with the guerrillas themselves.[40]

It is true that the state attracts many people as guards by providing them with generous salaries and benefits. Widespread unemployment and the extreme difficulty in earning a living may tempt some persons into doing such work. It is also well known that others are forced into being guards. This policy also serves to further spread and deepen the policy of divide, rule, and destroy. Nevertheless, despite the various factors which influence people into becoming guards, I still think that the presence of thousands of such guards throughout Kurdistan is a major indication of the weakness of Kurdish society. In the end, these guards are still Kurds and what they are doing is trying to kill, intimidate and terrorize other Kurds who desire equality, freedom, and a descent standard of living. The village guards must be one of the greatest weaknesses of Kurdish society. The fact that even after having been unmasked by the Turkish press, this institution is still in operation can only be related to the illnesses and weaknesses of Kurds. There have always been certain individuals who collaborate with imperialist and colonialist forces in every national liberation struggle. What makes the situation in Kurdistan different is that it is a mass phenomenon, which can only be explained by the lack of patriotic sentiment on the part of a certain sectors of the Kurdish population.

No matter how consistently these guards execute their functions as collaborators, agents, assistants, et al, they are still under constant state security and control. In some cases, it actually becomes imperative for the state to eliminate them due to the fact that they know too much about the illegal practices, tortures, and mass slaughters carried out by state forces.

Having cooperated with the latter in doing so much dirty work, they then become a liability, because they could leak information, for example, on the location of mass graves and similar places. However, the state never has any trouble in doing away with them; their deaths can always be explained as the result of battles with the PKK. I would like to relate a few examples from Kurdish history. The first comes from the Sheikh Said rebellion.

We can separate the tribal chiefs, sheikhs, and landlords during the 1925 rebellion into four categories: 1) those who participated directly in the movement, 2) those who took the side of the Turkish government, 3) those who were in the area but stayed out of the movement, and 4) those who were outside of the region of rebellion as well as the movement.

All except for 5-6 sheikhs who had taken part in the Hamidiye Cavalry were in the first group. The second group included the Norsin, Kufrevi, and Hizan sheikhs, Cemil Ceto in Garzan, Emin Rananli in Batman, etc. The third group consisted of those in the Zilan region. In the fourth category were Kurds from other regions.

There is an interesting point I would like to make here. Both those sheikhs who participated in the movement with all their heart and soul, as well as those who assisted the state in suppressing the movement were either executed or exiled. Cemil Ceto, for instance, was of great assistance to the central authorities, and even exchanged letters with Mustafa Kemal in which they both addressed each other as "brother." Nevertheless, he was neither able to save himself from execution nor his family from exile.

The 1925 Kurdish rebellion spread to Bitlis as well, and the Bitlis governor even fell captive in the hands of the rebels. The combined efforts of the Norsin and Kufrevi sheikhs, however, were able to break the rebellion and rescue the governor, after which they themselves were sent into exile. The same Norsin and Kufrevi sheikhs who had enabled the crushing of the rebellion were then banished and forced to remain within the confines of the Konya area. Unable to accept the way they were being rewarded after their invaluable assistance to the state, they tried over and over again to explain their situation any to authorities they could find.

During the time these sheikhs were in confinement in Konya, the former Bitlis governor happened to be appointed governor of that city, whereupon all the exiles formed a delegation and went to pay him a visit. The following is approximately the conversation that took place:

—Mr. Governor, we are [they recited their names]. We think you know we have been banished here to Konya.

—That's right.

—You know we did not take part in the rebellion and that we aided the state forces in suppressing it.

—Yes, I do know that.

—In fact we were the ones who rescued you from the rebelling Kurds.

—I know.

—Haven't you reported this to Ankara?

—I have.

—Since you and Ankara both know, then why are we being kept here?

—We did this as a favor to you. We could have executed you. This is the way we look at it—you were strong then. You suppressed the rebellion with your strength. You are still strong. How do I know you won't use your power on the side of the rebels next time round? We had to exile you. On the other hand, you fought against your own people. How can the government have any confidence in persons who fight against their own people?

Persons in the third category were both massacred and exiled. For example, although the Zilan valley was not in the region of the rebellion, for instance, many people there were massacred, and the rest exiled. Even some members of the fourth category, who had absolutely nothing to do with the event, were exiled or punished.

A number of Kurds who had operated against the state during the rebellion fled to Syria. Although court cases were initiated against them, they were not able to be tried due to their absence. Later, after the Democrat Party came to power in 1950, an amnesty was issued, which allowed them to return.

Following passage of a resolution in 1947, those who had been exiled to various regions in western Turkey also returned to their homes. They were given three alternatives:

a) They could remain in the west.

b) They could turn their property in the west over to the National Treasury and get new land from the National Treasury wherever they chose to resettle.

c) They could sell their property in the west and buy new property wherever they chose to resettle.

This was the situation for peasants. The Baban tribe, for instance, requested land from the National Treasury on the skirts of Nemrut mountain, where they then established the village of Soğurt (Tatvan). Landlords, sheikhs, and tribal chiefs returned to their former lands.

The second instance I would like to relate was reported by Sheikh Said's grandson, Melik Fırat. He relates that, while in exile in Thrace between 1936-1947, his uncle, Sheikh Ali Rıza Efendi, was visited by Kazim Dirik, who had been governor of the region where the Sheikh Said rebellion took place. Kazim Dirik is reported to have said that during the heat of the rebellion, three sheikhs from different tribes approached him as a group, saying that in exchange for 50,000 gold pieces they would fight against the rebellion. Dirik transferred the request to the government, who refused. Upon the repeated insistence of the sheikhs, however, they later decided to accept the offer and Dirik paid the sheikhs the amount requested. The latter then helped to crush the rebellion. Once all traces of the rebellion had been suppressed, he called them back, extracted twice the amount of money he had given them, and sent them all into exile.

A third incident has to do with the Sasson events of the 1930s. Emin-i Perihani of the Raman tribe was involved in close collaboration with the government at this time, even going so far as to turn his own brothers who were participants in the movement over to the authorities. The latter were then arrested and hung. One of them had to hide in the chicken coop while he was being searched for. Emin-i Perihan, who knew he was hiding in the chicken coop, drew him out to turn him over to the commanding officer. At the time, his brother said to him, "Ez firavin bim, ti sivi" ("I may be their lunch, but you will be their dinner.") That is exactly what happened. As soon as the rebellion was suppressed, the first thing the state did was to send Emin-i Perihani before the firing squad. The reason for this was that, having participated in secret state operations, he knew too much and constituted a potential danger. Besides, the state had no confidence in a man who would go so far as to turn his own brother over to be executed.

Finally, a fourth instance I would like to relate took place during the 1937-38 Dersim Uprising, at which time the state used all possible means to enlist the cooperation of Kurds close to those who were leading the rebellion. One of those they tried to win over was Rayber, the nephew of the leader of the movement, Seyid Rıza. A military official maintained close contact with him, paying him generously for any information he provided. Since Rayber was closely related to the leader of the movement, the state was able to receive much valuable information concerning plans, the names of participants, the shifting of forces within the region, etc. This was how they were able to murder Alisher, one of the movement's leaders, whom they took by surprise while resting in a house one day. His wife and infant were murdered along with him.

Rayber betrayed his people in countless of other ways for which he was amply rewarded. In 1938, once the last center of resistance had been thoroughly crushed, the government carried out one final operation, which was a top-secret raid on Rayber's home, where the latter was murdered before he even realized what was going on. His house was thoroughly searched, where all the different items he had been given for his services, such as gold plates and coins, gold cigarette holders and lighters, etc. were gathered up one by one. Word was then spread that he had been killed by bandits.

When you think about it, there is really nothing unusual in this. It is obvious that the state will not give those who have taken part in so much dirty work, and who know so many details about the state's illegal operations, long to live. The more they know, the sooner they will be eliminated by attributing their deaths to bandits, and their cases will be closed.

Following this incident, Kurdish children were no longer given the name Rayber, and those whose names were already Rayber were changed.

The organization of village guards by the state was unable to prevent the spread of the guerrilla movement. This led the government to give further duties to the guards beyond the scope of their agreements. According to the latter, the guards were supposed to protect the villagers against "brigands," which meant guerrillas, and report the situation to security forces. In addition, they were to act as guides for the security forces in their localities, showing them such things as caves or other possible hideouts. Eventually, however, the government began to force the guards to actually go up in the mountains and fight against the "brigands." They also try to transfer them outside of their own districts, and if they refuse, their salaries are taken back. Lately the government has begun considering arming the tribes to fight against the PKK. This is the latest example of how the state tries to preserve these feudal institution to prevent the spread of the Kurdish national movement.

How Can The Division of the Nation be Overcome?

It is said that the main reason Kurds have not been able to succeed and have been frequent victims of genocide and massacres is their lack of a progressive leadership. A feudal mentality is still present in the different organizations. The sheikhs, landlords, and tribal chiefs are an obstacle to the success of the national liberation movement. Rather than being self-sufficient, Kurds are always relying on one state or another to back them in their struggle against another state. With the increasing influence of

Marxism-Leninism in their organizations, however, the rate of success is on the upswing.

In my opinion, all the above interpretations are insufficient and superficial. The main drawback where Kurdistan is concerned is the fact that it has been carved up by the imperialists in a way that no other nation in the world has been divided. The latest and most lethal weapons are tried out on Kurds, as, for instance, chemical weapons, which are used nowhere else in the world. There is international cooperation in all this as well; one state uses them while another stands up to say that no traces of their use have been found. On top of it all, neither of the states concerned allows the United Nations or other international institutions to investigate under the pretext that such an intervention constitutes "intervention in internal affairs."[41]

The fact that the Kurdistan National Liberation Struggle is entirely surrounded by hostile forces, and that Kurdistan is colonized by more than one state makes the issue differ from any other. For these reasons, for example, it does not resemble the Palestinian issue. Given these heavily adverse circumstances, it is unfair to attribute the various problems to Kurdish organizations. It is always an easy way out. When it comes to self-reliance, we can say that Kurds are certainly fighting for the liberation of their homeland and possession of their own wealth; not to wrench it from the hands of one power to turn it over to another. No people fights for such a purpose. The Kurds, however, are in search of allies in their struggle. The fact that in this search they enter into unsound alliances is a matter stemming from the division of the nation.

The following questions must be asked: Why have not countries such as China, the Soviet Union, Albania, and the Eastern European countries assisted the Kurdish nation in its struggle for self-determination? Since the division of Kurdistan was brought about to benefit imperialism, why have the above nations pretended to be unaware of the problem? Why have these socialist countries even gone so far as to provide the reactionary, fascist, racist and colonialist state [*i.e.* Iraq] with arms which they knew would be used in Kurdistan? Moreover, it is a known fact that there are at least 30 Soviet experts whose position is to advise the Iraqi army on the use of chemical weapons. This tells us why the Soviet Union does not denounce Saddam Hussein for his frequent use of chemical weapons against the Kurds. There are many other such questions which need to be raised.

What can be done to overcome the tragic situation in which the Kurds are today entrenched? In my opinion there are three major ways. One is to increase the number of scientific studies being carried out on Kurdish society. The Kurds have a great need for science. The histories of the Middle East, Turkey, Iraq, Iran, and Syria must be rewritten. The development of scientific research will accelerate the development of national consciousness. The second way is to develop and spread the possibilities for writing and speaking Kurdish. The spread of written Kurdish is especially important. The most important way to overcome the boundaries drawn by the imperialists is the spread of Kurdish writing in a single standardized alphabet. The third way is to deal with the issue on an international level.

A glance at the political and social developments of the Middle East in the last ten years show us that every state, including the USA, France, Germany, etc. has some kind of policy on the Kurdish issue. The Kurds have become a significant factor in the political and military developments of the Middle East. To what degree these policies work for or against Kurds is another matter, and one that needs to be taken up. In any case, the Kurds have become a force to be reckoned with. When we examine the issue of a Kurdish alphabet, we see just how deep and extensive the international colonialist system in Kurdistan really is. In Turkey the Latin alphabet is used, in Iran, Iraq, and Syria the Arabic alphabet is used, and in the Soviet Union the Cyrillic alphabet is used. Even if writing and speaking Kurdish does become more widespread, the fact that in different regions, different alphabets are employed will prevent the formation of unity on the subject.

Experts say that the Latin alphabet is the most suitable one for writing Kurdish.

In the 1930s Hüsrev Gerede, Turkey's ambassador to Iran, explained to the Shah that, as their two countries were "common enemies" of the Kurds, they should make it a point to fortify the friendship between them. A joint military operation was planned against the Kurds by the two countries at the time.[42]

All the agreements between Turkey and Iraq have always been of such a nature. This is the inevitable result of this bilateral, sometimes even trilateral diplomacy. In reality, however, the Kurdish issue is of an international nature and should be dealt by international institutions where Kurdish representatives are also present. This may lead the states which colonize Kurdistan to complain of intervention in their internal affairs, but such a perspective is entirely subjective. Iraq, for example, does not complain about the frequent operations carried out by the Turkish army inside Iraqi borders. Apparently such operations are not considered to be unwanted intervention. When a United Nations delegation wished to examine the results of the use of chemical weapons in Southern Kurdistan, however, they were refused permission on the grounds that such an investigation constituted intervention in the internal affairs of the country.

One of the most important ways to change the negative conditions which have been imposed on the Kurds is through the development of scientific studies which will ensure a sounder approach to the Kurdish problem as well as develop a keener political awareness of it. The debates which will arise in conjunction with these studies will raise Kurdish national consciousness and develop the character of Kurdish society.[43]

This is why it is necessary to emphasize the importance of scientific studies on the subject. Prof. Fuad Köprülü points out the following on the historical ties between science and ideology. "The false representations of history for the sake of political interests or in defence of diseased ideologies is a painful and useless insult to science and human dignity. But let us say with pleasure that such movements are transitory, and that in spite of everything, the number of scientists seeking objective reality is increasing all over the world."[44]

The fact that Dr. Fuad Köprülü has made such a statement does not necessarily mean that he observes it! In saying this, I believe that Prof. Fuad Köprülü was criticizing researchers in the Eastern Bloc countries. In truth, however, he, as well as many others like him, have done exactly that in Turkey. They have falsely represented history "for the sake of political interests" with their defence of the official Turkish state ideology. In Turkey, everything possible has been done to hide the existence of the Kurds in history and present these people as a small and insignificant group. However, this practice is not diminishing, as Prof. Köprülü would have us believe. On the contrary it is increasing. In countries such as Turkey, where the official state ideology is dominant and accepted as scientific knowledge, it has become a permanent factor in universities and scientific research centers.

What, of course, should exist, is for scientific activity to be carried on properly, with all persons carrying out research and studies in relation to Kurdistan absolutely freely in their thoughts and actions. Such persons should not wait for the development of a democratic environment before carrying out their studies.

People who always observe the official state ideology and laws are never able to think and act freely. Researchers must be able to carry out their work without feeling such restrictions, and they must heed their results.

To give a specific example, let's imagine one is studying the Kurdish movement following the establishment of the Turkish Republic, and all of one's material comes from official sources. What about Kurdish sources published by various Kurdish institutions in Europe? Shouldn't these sources be taken into account as well? But doing so may constitute an offence under Turkish law.

This is why freedom is so essential for scientific procedure. Freedom is the essential element for sound research. No research can exist without this dimension. The information which has been produced on Kurdistan to date is insufficient and incorrect. This is a result of the policies followed by countries which mutually colonize Kurdistan. Any documents or material which would reveal the truth have either been destroyed or made inaccessible.

This brings us to another point, which is that freedom is not a category only to be used against such institutions as the state, police, and courts. It must also be safeguarded against various political currents. Given the circumstances surrounding their existence, Kurds need to be very cautious on this point. Various Kurdish parties may find themselves supported by various states at different times for various reasons. This may lead members of that particular party to refrain from criticizing the particular state assisting them at the time. Again, this stands in the way of scientific procedure.

Conclusion

Kurdistan was divided at a time when the principle of the right of nations to self-determination was sweeping through Asia, the Middle East, and North Africa. The attitude of the Bolsheviks on this issue during the 1917 revolution should be looked into. The rise and fall of the Mahabad Kurdish Republic in 1946 needs to be examined. Such research will enrich our knowledge on Kurdistan and the Middle East. Simple repetition of what Lenin and Stalin had to say on the right of nations to self-determination is of no use if one does not ask the questions posed above. In reality, the writings of Lenin and Stalin on this subject were not completely put into practice. The events which have taken place in the Soviet Union, Romania, Bulgaria, Yugoslavia and China are a clear indication of this. It is a major duty of socialists to examine thoroughly why the reality differs from the theory.

It is not a solution to make such proposals regarding the Kurdish question today as "...with the working class as vanguard...." We need to understand why the Turkish working class has always taken the government's side when it comes to the Kurds, and has never come out in support of the revolutionary and democratic rights of the Kurds.

One can still hear it be said in Turkey that Kemalism was the spark for the liberation of all the oppressed nations of the East and raised the beacon for the liberation of all the enslaved and colonial nations of the world. Given Kemalism's role in the division of Kurdistan, how can such propaganda still be maintained?

Saddam Hussein's ability to use chemical warfare against Kurds with such ease and lack of concern needs to be thought about. Why isn't Israel able to use the same methods against the Palestinians? Why does Saddam Hussein's fascist, colonialist, and racist regime enjoy Soviet support? Reports should be prepared concerning the relations between U.S. secret services and the Kurds, and the USSR must take a more active stance on the matter. What about the 30 Soviet experts on chemical warfare stationed in Iraq? Why are they there?

Protests and demonstrations were arranged in various cities around the world to denounce the Iraqi regime for its use of chemical warfare against the Kurds. In Turkey, however, permission for such demonstrations was refused, and the police chased off or arrested anyone who attempted to protest or denounce the regime of Saddam Hussein. This solidarity and cooperation between the Iraqi and Turkish governments must be questioned and exposed.

What I am trying to make clear is that science and politics are two very different fields of activity. There must be no concessions in science. Scientists must resist giving in to the pressures of the official Turkish ideology and the state laws. Politics is different. People involved in politics may grant concessions, in accordance with the situation. Persons and institutions involved in politics must be made aware of the need for independent centers for scientific research. This is something which will be of great benefit to Kurdistan in the long run.

On the other hand, information collected on Kurdistan must not be confused with propositions made for the solution of the Kurdish issue. The concept of Kurdistan as a "colony," for instance, has been very useful for the interpretation of the historical development of Kurdish society. Certain Turkish left organizations, however, reject this concept on the grounds that it lays the foundations for the formation of separate organizations (*i.e.* independent from those of the Turkish left). By doing so they are making a big mistake. Kurdistan, in fact, is a nation lacking even colonial status.

The studies carried out on Kurdistan can be used for various purposes. There is no doubt about their use for the very important goal of finding a revolutionary and democratic solution for the Kurdish issue. They can also, however, be used towards the realization of assimilation projects and for the prevention of the formation of a Kurdish social and political opposition. Of course, the ideas and attitude of researchers will vary according to their goals in mind, and in the second case, the research is likely to be carried out secretly and the results not to be published. The best thing to do, still, is to act in accordance with the needs of scientific methodology. The results must be published and made available for criticism, which is one of the best ways to ensure objectivity.

Prof. Dr. Yonah Alexander, specialist on international politics and terrorism at George Washington University, describes the Kurds as "a nation fighting for other bosses." Jill Hamburg, writing in the magazine *The Nation*, in an article entitled "A Forgotten People: the World and the Kurds" refers to the Kurds as "everybody's soldiers," and points out that they have always fought in the service of others, and have not been able to fight a strong war of national liberation.

Dr. Alexander, in a speech made at a seminar on "Terrorism in the Middle East and the Balance of Power" proposes the establishment of a pact between Turkey, Iraq and Israel to bring about a solution to the Kurdish issue.[45]

There are two ways to make use of such information. The first is to say, "Well, since the Kurds have always fought in the service of others, why don't we use them in the same way? Why don't we arm and incite them into fighting against those forces which are our enemies? Let's do everything possible to turn this into a dynamic process." Although such a policy is totally disrespectful of human rights, it is exactly what is being done by the intelligence services of the various nations which colonize Kurdistan.

On 28 August 1989, the same day Dr. Alexander's proposals for a pact against the Kurds were published in the newspaper *Sabah*, there was an important article in *Günaydin* newspaper concerning the mass poisoning of Kurdish refugees which took place at Kiziltepe camp in early June. This article pointed out that according to British Broadcasting Corporation, following an investigation carried out by the organization "International Medical Relief," there was clear evidence that the peshmergas had been poisoned by Iraqi agents who were still circulating freely about the camp. Organophosphates produced by mercury poisoning had been found in blood, urinary, and bread samples brought from the camp.

It should not be forgotten that these Kurds were forced to seek refuge in Turkey to save their lives. As soon as they came they were surrounded by barbed wire, observation towers, and police stations. Contact and aid from their relatives in Northern Kurdistan was forbidden. They were forbidden to work or leave the camp without permission. The water, bread, tents, and blankets provided were insufficient. No provisions were made for health care, nutrition, and the raising of their children. Iraqi agents were able to circulate freely about the camp and make agreements with the bakers so that they could put poison into the bread while it was being baked. Is it easy to poison thousands of people? Is it possible that this was done without the knowledge of the Turkish intelligence agencies? Likewise the bakers who put out the poisoned bread were not subjected to the slightest questioning. The matter was closed. This is an example of the convenience of the policy of divide and rule.

The right of self-determination must be granted to the Kurds. This is an absolute necessity. The Arabs, Persians, and Turks do not and never will govern the Kurds justly. They rule them and will always rule them through chemical and biological warfare, poisonous gasses, oppression, and tyranny. They frequently uproot them from their homes and banish them to the desert. They make use of all possible means to exterminate Kurdish identity. Exile, breaking up families, terrorizing children, forcing people to live in a state of panic.... They destroy Kurdistan's natural resources, including the forests and the fields, the animals and the birds, through chemicals and poisonous gasses. They reduce the forests to places where "not even weeds take root." Their spies and agents incite hostilities amongst the Kurds, furthering the policy of divide and rule. The smallest disputes are blown up and turned into blood feuds.

Although these are obviously bloody methods relying on state terror, why is there still insistence that the Kurds be ruled by the Arabs, Persians, and Turks? In future this state of affairs will become even more difficult due to the rapidly spreading national consciousness. By the end of the twentieth century it will no longer be possible to keep them as anyone's slaves. This consciousness can only be suppressed through violence and bloodshed. This makes the Kurds' right to self determination an objective necessity. It is the only possible way to do away with banishment, forced migration, life in camps surrounded by barbed wire, hunger, thirst and illness.

Moreover, even though they lasted short periods, there were times when Kurds ruled themselves. These times began to bring the Kurds peace and tranquillity. Let's take a look back at the late 1960s and early 1970s at the national liberation struggle led by Molla Mustafa Barzani in Southern Kurdistan. During this time social conflicts were resolved without the need to resort to arms and bloodshed. This period needs to be studied by all institutions dealing with the Kurdish issue. The short lived Mahabad Kurdish Republic of 1946 provided an environment where peace and freedom from conflict could flourish. These examples show how the Kurds can rule themselves more effectively, more justly, and in accordance with human rights.

During the period between 1840-1848, Kurdistan was also at peace under the rule of Jizre Emiri Bedirhan. There was justice. Those who broke up this order and were against it were the Ottomans, British, French, and Russians who were their collaborators.

The states which rule Kurdistan have a very different understanding of what peace means. For them it is to force the Kurds into a state where they can no longer breathe because of widespread oppression and violence. True peace, however, can only exist where there is freedom and equality—which means in the absence of state terror.

Some say that the Kurds have never been more than toys in the hands of imperialists. The various Middle Eastern governments have always used the Kurds as pawns in their own conflicts. Although people who espouse such views shed crocodile tears as they do so, in essence, they are doing nothing more than looking down on them. In reality, this deplorable situation is the natural result of the policy of divide and rule and the fact that Kurds have always been used by others. In order to come out against those who look down on them, and in order not to be used by others, once again, the development and spread of Kurdish national consciousness is imperative.

* * *

Epilogue

In June 1981, I was taken to Ankara police headquarters for interrogation. State terror was widespread in those days. On the third and last night of my stay at Ankara police headquarters a team from Adapazari came suddenly and took me in a car heading for Adapazari. There were two civilian policemen in the car, and both of them were Kurds. The one sitting beside me turned to me suddenly and said: "So how are you going to solve this problem?"

"What problem?"

"The Kurdish problem, the one you wrote about."

It was a dark night and the road was deserted. Besides, no one was informed that I had been arrested and was being taken to Adapazari. Feeling great fear and anxiety, I thought about how I should answer. The policeman repeated the question.

"Come on, tell us what you think. How are we going to solve this problem?"

"I've been carrying out research on Kurdish society, trying to understand and comprehend the Kurdish issue. Researchers are not required to propose solutions for social and political issues."

"But how do you think it should be solved?" he insisted.

"I'm conducting research. I'm trying to understand all aspects of the Kurdish issue."

He would not be satisfied with this answer, and pressed for something concrete. "So you have researched and researched, you've learned everything. So how can the problem be solved?"

The driver and the policeman in front kept silent while the one beside me increased his pressure.

"I haven't concluded my research, nor can I find time to do so. I keep getting arrested."

This went on for some time. He wouldn't give up. In the end I said, "Proposing a solution for the Kurdish issue is a political task. This is the work of political parties and organizations. Some of them call for an end to the repression of Kurdish language and culture, for Kurdish to be spoken and written freely, for Kurdish newspapers, radios, and TV, and for education in Kurdish. Others see this as insufficient. They may also call for Kurdish districts to be governed by Kurdish governors. Other groups may call for the formation of a separate state. Still others call for an independent, united and democratic Kurdistan comprised of Kurdistan as a whole. All these can be presented as solutions, and the strength of each varies according to the strength behind the social and political force which propose them. I don't have anything to say on this matter. I don't know how strong the different organizations are. I'll tell you this much; there are 166 states in the world today. I'd like Kurdistan to be the 167th. That's my personal desire, but political issues are not solved by voicing personal desires. A number of different states have interests in Kurdistan today, and they become uncomfortable by such proposals and want to prevent such things from developing no matter what the cost. We have to look at the facts."

After this our conversation came to an end. Nothing else was said until we reached Adapazari. While I spoke, the police just listened without interfering. They did not seem to be angry.

ENDNOTES

1. Utkan Kocatürk, *Atatürk'ün Fikir ve Düşünceleri* (Ankara: Turhan Kitabevi, 1984), p. 149.
2. *Milliyet*, 31 August 1930, quoted in Lucien Rambout, *Kurdistan, (1918-1946)*, (Istanbul: Komal Yayınevi, 1978), p. 41.
3. *Milliyet*, 19 September 1930, cited in Lucien Rambout, *op. cit.*, p. 41.
4. İsmet İnönü, *Hatıralar*, vol. 2, (Ankara: Bilgi Yayınevi, 1987), p. 202.
5. *Cumhuriyet*, 28 September 1989.
6. *e.g.*, Ord. Prof. Dr. Sulhi Dönmezer, "Equality of Citizens in Turkey," in *Yeni Forum*, no. 224, 1-15 January, 1989, p. 22-23.
7. *2000'e Doğru*, no. 25, 18 June 1989, p. 24.
8. "Türkiye Halkları, Yakın Tarihimizden İhanetler," *Cumhurriyet*, 3-5 February 1970.
9. "Dünün ve Bugünün Defterleri" *Türkiye Sorunları*, 1 July 1988, p. 14.
10. Behçet Cemal, *Şeyh Said İsyanı* (Istanbul: Hisar Matbaası, 1955), p. 19; Reşat Halli (ed.), *Türkiye Cumhuriyeti'nde Ayaklanmalar, 1924-1938* (Ankara: Genelkurmay Başkanliği Yayınevi, 1972), p. 79.
11. *Devrimci Doğu Kültür Ocakları Dava Dosyası* (Ankara: Komal Yayınevi, 1975), pp. 113-277, 305-317).
12. İsmail Beşikçi, *Bilim Yöntemi, Türkiye'deki Uygulama 3. Cumhuriyet Halk Firkası'nin Tüzüğü* (1927) *ve Kürt Sorunu* (Istanbul: Komal Yayınevi, 1978), pp. 243-278.
13. Parts of this survey were published in F. W. Frey, *The Turkish Political Elite* (Cambridge, Mass., 1965).
14. İsmail Beşikçi, op. cit., p. 275.
15. *2000'e Doğru*, no. 25, 18 June 1989, p. 24; *Medya Güneşi*, no. 9, May-June 1989, p. 25.
16. In 1985 a book was published by the Research Institute for Turkish Culture with the title "The Place of Eastern Anatolia within the Overall Turkish Nation" (*Türk Milli Bütünlüğü Içinde Doğu Anadolu*). The book was prepared by Prof. Dr. Bahaeddin Ögel, Prof. Dr. Haluk Dursun Yıldız, Dr. M. Fahreddin Kirzioğlu, Prof. Dr. Mehmet Eröz, Prof. Dr. Bayram Kodaman, and Dr. Abdülhalik Çay.
17. *2000'e Doğru*, no. 1, 4-10 January 1987.
18. *2000'e Doğru*, no. 52, 20-26 December 1987.
19. At this point it is necessary to reconsider the meaning of internationalism. In late 1974 the Kurds, while waging the struggle for national liberation against the regime of Saddam Hussein in Southern Kurdistan, downed two Iraqi planes over the mountains of Kurdistan. A newspaper in Turkey printed a photograph of one of the wrecked Mig planes surrounded by a group of Kurdish children.

20. Mihri Belli, "Anılar," *Milliyet*, 20 June 1989 - 3 July 1989. Koray Düzgören (ed.).
21. Sinan Doğru, "Ölümünün 30 Yildönümünde Dr. Şekif Hüsnü Deymer'i Anmaya Çagrı" ("Sefik Hüsnü and Social Chauvinism") *Medya Güneşi*, no. 8, April 1989, pp. 32-33; "Zorunlu Bir Açiklama" ("An Obligatory Statement,") *Ozgür Gelecek,"* no. 8, July 1989, p. 14; Sinan Doğru, "Özgür Gelecek'in 'Zorunlu Açıklama'sı üzerine" ("On the Obligatory Statement of *Özgür Gelecek,*") *Medya Güneşi*, no. 10, July-August 1989, pp. 63-64.
22. *Saçak*, no. 25, February 1986, p. 30.
23. Uğur Mumcu, "Bu Ne Bencillik?" *Cumhuriyet*, 19 November 1983.
24. *Cumhuriyet*, 13 October 1984. See also Uğur Mumcu, "Azınlık Şovenizmi," *Cumhuriyet*, 2 September 1984.
25. For other articles where this and related concepts see: Alpaslan Türkeş, *Temel Görüşler* (Istanbul: Dergah Yayınları, 3rd ed., 1976), p. 35; Turhan Feyzioğlu, *Milliyet* (Istanbul: Dergah Yayınları, 1975), pp. 243-250; Ahmet Kabaklı, "Komşu Hakkı," *Tercüman,* 6 October 1985; Ahmet Kabaklı, "Eşkıya Alçaktır," *Tercüman*, 12-13 October 1985; İlhan Bardakçı, "Çukurdaki Kahpe," *Tercüman,* 13 October 1984; Ergün Göze, "Hakkari'den Ingiltere'ye Kadar, Yahut Yalancının Mumu," *Tercüman*, 15 October 1984; Coşkun Kirca, "Milli Birlik Ortamı," *Hürriyet*, 6 March 1987; Coşkun Kırca, "Diller, Dilcikler," *Hürriyet*, 11 March 1987; Rauf Tamer, "Bu Adam Ne Diyor?" *Tercüman*, 7 January 1985; Rauf Tamer, "Tepkiler," *Tercüman*, 12 January 1985.
26. Coşkun Kirca, *ibid.*
27. There is an anecdote which is useful in portraying the role of the horse in the wars between the indigenous population and the Spanish and Portuguese invaders. Both sides were preparing to fight on a large battlefield. All the indigenous warriors were grouped around their chiefs. As the fighting broke out, one of these chiefs attacked one of the invaders, who, in addition to being on horseback, had both a gun and a sword. The indigenous chief wounded the invader's horse, who had to leave the battlefield, so that his rider was left fighting on foot. The chief, who had not realized that the horse and the man were two separate beings, was thunderstruck, thinking that the person he had killed was some kind of divine creature who had returned to life. He threw down his weapon, and along with the other indigenous warriors ceased to fight. The invaders then took advantage of the fact that all the indigenous men were in a state of panic and cut them all to ribbons with their swords. See Eduardo Galeano, *The Open Veins of Latin America: Five Centuries of the Pillage of a Continent* (New York: Monthly Review Press), New York 1973.
28. İsmail Beşikci, *Bilim Yöntemi, Turkiye'deki Uygulama I, Kürtlerin Mecburi Iskani* (Istanbul: Komal Yayınevi, 1977), p. 79.

29. Regarding the Trial of the 49, see *Medya Güneşi*, no. 1, April 1988, p. 46-47. For the names of the 49 persons see Fevzi Bilge, "Siyasal Tarinimizden bir Kesit." The name of Serafettin Elçi, however, has been omitted from the list and another name listed twice. Dr. Naci Kutlay, who is himself one of the 49, has written a serious study on the 49 where he stresses the need for further such studies. See Dr. Naci Kutlay, "30. Yilinda 49'lar Olayi," *Bergeh* 1/1989, pp. 29-41. *Bergeh* is a Kurdish-Turkish magazine published in Sweden.
30. Regarding the Trial of the 23, see *Bir Kürt Devrimcisi Edip Karahan'in Anisina,* (Istanbul: Komal Yayınları, 1977), p. 89-136.
31. Tahsin Saraç, "Yaşamın Oykusunden Değinmeler," *Turkiye Yazilari*, 11 February 1978, p. 22-29.
32. "Doğu'ya Neden Özel Sektör Yatırımı Yok?," *2000'e Doğru*, no. 46, 6 November 1988.
33. *Mem-u Zin* was first published by Mehmet Emin Bozarslan in 1968 (Gün Yayınevi, Istanbul). In this edition, the Kurdish original was printed on one page, with the Turkish translation on the facing page. The twelve couplets mentioned above were not included. I wanted very much to take them up in the present work; unfortunately I was unable to get hold of the text. Nevertheless, I would like to take the opportunity to relate an incident from my own past which I believe will shed light on very different aspects of the Kurdish issue.
34. Immediately after *Mem-u Zin* was published, another version was published under the name *Mem-o Zin*. The author of the book was said to be a man named Ahmet Faik, and the story was written in Turkish and presented as a Turkish legend. Shortly afterwards, however, the book disappeared. I believe the MIT was responsible both for its publication and its disappearance. This is a prime example of the cultural imperialism applied in Kurdistan. A comparison of the two versions would bring out the fraudulent misrepresentations which were carried out in the latter publication.
35. On the other hand the opposite case can also be made. For example, the people refer to the PKK guerillas who die in action against Turkish security forces as "martyrs." The people claim the dead guerillas and bury them with ceremonies. Visits of condolence to their families go on for weeks despite police harassment and repression. The security forces are against Kurds claiming the bodies of such "brigands" and "bandits." They want the bodies to remain unclaimed to create the impression that the movement has no popular support.
36. A study of the present condition of Kurds in relation to their ethnic roots would be a worthy undertaking. Their relation to Gutis, Assyrians, Urartians, and Medes needs to be brought to light. We know the Gutis and later the Medes to have been ancestors of the Kurds. The Urartians are closely related to Armenians.

37. Ziya Gökalp, *Kürt Aşiretleri Üzerinde Sosyolojik Araştırmalar*, Istanbul: Komal Yayınları, 1976.
38. Süleyman Uludağ (ed.), *Mukaddima 1, 2*, (Istanbul: Dergah Yayınları, 1988), pp. 496-499.
39. "Doğu'da Jirkilerle Anlaşma, Devletin Umudu Kanun Kaçaklar," *2000'e Doğru*, no. 2, 22 May 1988, pp. 8-15; "SHP'nin Korucularla Ilgili Raporu," *Milliyet*, 10 August 1987; Yalçin Dogan, "Doğu'da Kürdü Kürde Kirdirma Operasyonu!," *Sabah*, 15 August 1989.
40. Evin Aydar, Selami Ince, Ökkes Tavus, "Siirt-Adiyaman Korucuları Kelle Avcıları," *2000'e Doğru*, 11 June 1989, no. 24, pp. 20-23; "Siirt'te Korucu Terörü, Eruh'da Parçalanmiş Ceset," *2000'e Doğru*, p. 26, 25 June 1989, pp. 16-18.
41. Hüsrev Gerede, *Siyasi Hatıralarım I, Iran (1930-1934)* (Istanbul: Vakit Basımevi), 1952, pp. 68-69.
42. We have made it clear that one of the major differences between Kurdistan and a colony, in the classical sense of the term, is the lack of recognition of Kurdish identity and the effort made to destroy this identity. We experience this every day, especially in radio and TV news. The Kurdish refugees who entered Turkey in August 1988 were continually referred to as "those who escaped Iraq" and in similar terms, rather than as Kurds, because to call them Kurdish would have meant recognition of their identity.
43. W. Barthold-F. Köprülü, *Islam Medeniyeti Tarihi* (Ankara: Diyanet Işleri Başkanlığı Yayınları, 1963, 2nd ed.), pp. xxii-xxi.
44. There is a big difference between carrying out research on Kurdistan and proposing solutions to the Kurdish issue. In this respect, studies on Kurdistan should not be immediately linked to propositions for the solution of the issue. Proposal for solutions and action are political and ideological activities related to the social and political strength of the organizations which make them. The strength of the proposals have to do with the political and social strength of whoever makes them. Production of information on Kurdistan is a scientific activity which requires no political or social strength. Anyone can do this on their own.
45. *Sabah*, 28 August 1989.

APPENDIX

Political Parties and Their Kurdish or Turkish Acronyms

Kurdistan Workers' Party (Partiya Karkari Kurdistan or PKK)

Motherland Party (Anavatan Partisi or ANAP)

National Intelligence Agency (MIT)

National Order Party (Milli Nizam Partisi or MNP)

National Salvation Party (Milli Selamet Partisi or MSP)

Nationalist Action Party (Milliyetçi Hareket Partisi or MHP)

Prosperity Party (Refah Partisi or RP)

Republican Peoples Party (Cumhuriyet Halk Partisi or CHP)

Social Democratic Populist Party (Sosyal Demokrat Halk Partisi SHP)

Turkish Workers Party (Türkiye İşçi Partisi or TIP)

True Path Party (Doğru Yol Partisi or DYP)

www.ingramcontent.com/pod-product-compliance
Ingram Content Group UK Ltd.
Pitfield, Milton Keynes, MK11 3LW, UK
UKHW020141250726
13967UKWH00002B/796